Zaner-Bloser
Handwriting

On the Road to Writing and Reading

for PreKindergarten

Design and Illustration
The Artifact Group

ISBN-13: 978-0-7367-5365-4
ISBN-10: 0-7367-5365-6

D1508441

Zaner-Bloser, Inc., P.O. Box 16764, Columbus, Ohio 43216-6764 (1-800-421-3018)

www.zaner-bloser.com

Printed in United States of America

11 (330) 5 4 3

Table of Contents Teacher Guide

Table of Contents *Music, Mazes & More CD-ROM*

Sing-Along Songs

Track	Title	Skill
Track 1:	Sky-Writing	Letter Formation
Track 2:	ABC Rap	Letter Recognition
Track 3:	Top to Bottom	Spatial Awareness
Track 4:	Wake Up Fingers	Fine Motor (Finger Warm-Up)
Track 5:	Thumbs Up	Fine Motor (Finger Warm-Up)
Track 6:	Thumbkin	Fine Motor (Finger Warm-Up)
Track 7:	My Two Hands	Fine Motor
Track 8:	Hold Your Crayon	Writing Position
Track 9:	I Pull Down	Basic Writing Stroke
Track 10:	Slide Along	Basic Writing Stroke
Track 11:	Circle Song	Basic Writing Stroke
Track 12:	Slant Dance	Basic Writing Stroke

Music, Mazes & More CD-ROM

On the Road to Writing and Reading for PreKindergarten

Helps young children develop fundamental prewriting skills and prepare for success in Kindergarten and beyond!

On the Road to Writing and Reading is a developmentally-appropriate program that introduces young children to written communication. Through songs and stories, rhythm and rhyme, movement and manipulatives, the activities will complement any PreKindergarten curriculum.

Who better than Zaner-Bloser?

Zaner-Bloser, the nation's leading provider of handwriting instruction for more than 100 years, has combined experience, research, and proven instructional methods into fun, simple-to-use materials for young children.

Kit Box

Kit includes:

- Teacher Guide
- *Music, Mazes & More* CD-ROM (included in Teacher Guide)
- Group Time Cards
- Alphabet Cards
- Take-Home Alphabet Posters (English and Spanish)
- Wikki Stix®
- Touch and Trace Manuscript Letter Cards
- Magnetic Dry-Erase Board and Letters
- Story Journals

Teacher Guide

Music, Mazes & More CD-ROM

Sing-Along Songs

Twelve sing-along songs are performed by award-winning early childhood educator and performer Debbie Clement. With more than twenty-five years of experience working with young children, Debbie brings her love of music, movement, rhythm, and rhyme to age-appropriate songs developed to introduce prereading, prewriting, and letter formation to young children.

Optional Writing Readiness Pages

Printable practice pages help young children develop prewriting and handwriting skills.

Mazes

Mazes at three levels of difficulty help build fine-motor skills, eye-hand coordination, and crayon/pencil control.

Picture and Letter Cards

Cut-apart cards can be used for letter recognition and sound-symbol awareness through matching and sorting games.

Basic Strokes

Children practice basic strokes through pictures and writing.

Letters and Numerals

Children trace and write letters and numerals.

Sing-Along Song Lyrics

Print the song lyrics to use in the classroom or to send home to parents.

Group Time Cards

Alphabet Cards

Take-Home Alphabet Posters (English and Spanish)

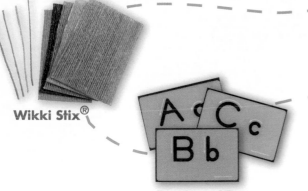

Wikki Stix®

Touch and Trace Manuscript Letter Cards

Magnetic Dry-Erase Board and Letters

Story Journal

The Instructional Plan

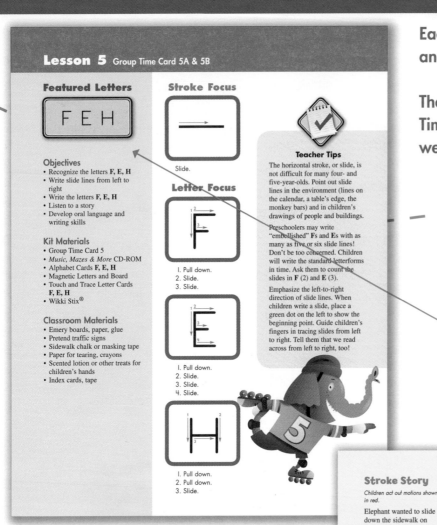

Featured Letters

F E H

Objectives
- Recognize the letters **F, E, H**
- Write slide lines from left to right
- Write the letters **F, E, H**
- Listen to a story
- Develop oral language and writing skills

Kit Materials
- Group Time Card 5
- *Music, Mazes & More* CD-ROM
- Alphabet Cards **F, E, H**
- Magnetic Letters and Board
- Touch and Trace Letter Cards **F, E, H**
- Wikki Stix®

Classroom Materials
- Emery boards, paper, glue
- Pretend traffic signs
- Sidewalk chalk or masking tape
- Paper for tearing, crayons
- Scented lotion or other treats for children's hands
- Index cards, tape

Stroke Focus

Slide.

Letter Focus

F
1. Pull down.
2. Slide.
3. Slide.

E
1. Pull down.
2. Slide.
3. Slide.
4. Slide.

H
1. Pull down.
2. Pull down.
3. Slide.

Teacher Tips

The horizontal stroke, or slide, is not difficult for many four- and five-year-olds. Point out slide lines in the environment (lines on the calendar, a table's edge, the monkey bars) and in children's drawings of people and buildings.

Preschoolers may write "embellished" **F**s and **E**s with as many as five or six slide lines! Don't be too concerned. Children will write the standard letterforms in time. Ask them to count the slides in **F** (2) and **E** (3).

Emphasize the left-to-right direction of slide lines. When children write a slide, place a green dot on the left to show the beginning point. Guide children's fingers in tracing slides from left to right. Tell them that we read across from left to right, too!

Each unit covers one week of instruction and focuses on two or three letters.

The easy 3-step lesson plan for Group Time, Center Time, and Play Time works well in the PreK environment.

The **lesson opener** page lists objectives and materials, gives stroke descriptions for focus letters, and offers teaching tips on helping young children with letter formation.

Interactive **Stroke Story** opens Group Time activities on Day 1.

Step-by-step instructions for using the **Group Time Cards** on Days 1 and 2.

Stroke Story

Children act out motions shown in red.

Elephant wanted to slide down the sidewalk on roller-skates like his cousin. Grandma said it was his turn to try the skates.

"Will I fall down?" he asked Grandma.

"You might fall down while you are learning," she said. "Here, put these on to protect you."

She gave him a sturdy helmet, knee pads, and elbow and wrist pads. Elephant put them on, first the helmet (pretend to strap on helmet), then the knee pads (put on knee pads), then the elbow and wrist pads (put on elbow and wrist pads).

"Wait," said Elephant, and he ran inside. When he came out, he had two more hats on top of his helmet.

"You don't need those," Grandma laughed.

"Yes, I do," Elephant said. "With three hats, I'll be super safe!"

Elephant put a skate on his left foot (put on skate), then his right foot (put on skate). He stood up quickly, and fell down just as quickly (fall down).

"It's OK," said Grandma. "Try again." Elephant stood (stand up). He turned his body to the right and slid one foot forward, then the other. He didn't fall! He slid again carefully. He was doing it! (Slide several times from left to right.) Elephant kept trying until he could slide smoothly along.

Group Time Days 1–2

*Gather children together for group time. Use the **Group Time** information on pages 16–17 and the notes below.*

Group Time Card 5A
1. Warm up with a song. Choose one listed at right.
2. Tell the Stroke Story.
3. Trace the arrow under the elephant from left to right. Say "slide".
4. Sing "ABC Rap." Point to the target letters in yellow on the Alphabet Road.
5. Sky-write each slide line in **F, E,** and **H.** For each, say "slide".

Group Time Card 5B
1. Warm up with a song. Choose one listed at right.
2. Sing "ABC Rap." Point to the letters on the Alphabet Road. Clap when you come to **F, E,** and **H.**

3. Talk about the letter shapes. They look like parts of a ladder. **F** can be found inside **E.** Who has these letters in his or her name? Can these letters be found in the room? Read the word for each letter. Find the letter in the word.
4. Sky-write each letter several times, beginning at the green dot and following the arrows. Say the name of each line aloud.
5. Write an uppercase message to Elephant, such as HOLD ON TO YOUR HATS, ELEPHANT, using shared or interactive writing. Read the message together, pointing to letters, words, and spaces.

38

Developmentally-appropriate activities cover the seven key prewriting skills that are the focus of the program.

Fun With Fundamentals

See pages 10–13 for more information about the development of these essential prewriting skills.

Developing Gross-Motor Skills

Use sidewalk chalk on the playground or strips of masking tape on the floor to form the letters **F, E,** and **H** at a large size. Place a green dot to show the starting position for each letter. Then invite children to swim like a Fish along the **F,** stomp like an Elephant along the **E,** and gallop like a Horse along the **H.**

Developing Fine-Motor Skills

Draw horizontal lines across paper for children to tear. Use a green dot to mark the left side of each line. Show how to secure the paper with the helper hand as the thumb and pointer finger of the dominant hand are used for tearing. Provide crayons so children can write their names on the torn paper strips.

Developing Spatial Awareness

Introduce children to their left hands. "Greet" each child's left hand. Throughout the day, give left hands special tasks to do and treats such as scented lotion, stickers, and interesting things to feel. Children can talk to their left hands, too. A few days later, give special attention to the right hand.

Developing Print Awareness

Act out reading and writing behaviors and have children tell you whether you are being a good reader/writer or not. For example, read the **ABCs** on the Group Time Card from right to left. *No, no, that's wrong,* the children will tell you. Write the slide lines in **E** from right to left. *No, that's not right either.* Write **F** and **H** correctly and get children's approval.

Developing Letter Recognition

Write **F, E,** or **H** on index cards. Tape one card to each child's back. Challenge children to ask each other questions that will help them guess their letter. They might ask, *How many slide lines does my letter have? How many pull down lines does my letter have? What sound does my letter make? What words have my letter?*

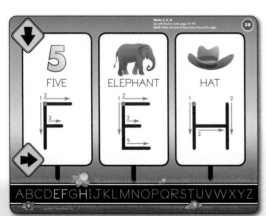

FIVE   ELEPHANT   HAT

F E H

ABCDEFGHIJKLMNOPQRSTUVWXYZ

39

Chant
Use this chant to help children remember how to hold their crayon when they draw or write.

Hold Your Crayon
Crayon, crayon,
Do you want to write?
Jump in my fingers.
I won't hold you tight.

Lean on tall friend,
Pointer on top,
Rest on my thumb,
I won't let you drop.

Ring and pinky
Tuck in beside.
They touch the paper
As we take a ride.

Center Time Days 3–5

*Choose multisensory activities for writing practice from the **Center Time** information on pages 18–19 or the activity below.*

Scratchy Letters Trace emery boards to make templates on sheets of paper for forming **F, E,** and **H.** Hint: Use two emery boards for vertical lines, so they are twice the length of horizontal lines. For example, use four boards to make **F**—two for the pull down line and two more for the slide lines. Children glue the boards on the templates to form letters. They use their fingers to trace each letter, saying "slide" for each slide line.

Play Time Days 3–5

*Use the **Play Time** information on page 20 and the idea below to introduce purposeful writing into children's dramatic play.*

Traffic If you have an area with a smooth floor, allow children to slide across it in their stocking feet. They can pretend to be driving cars or using roller skates as they slide. Provide materials for making traffic signs to regulate the travelers (LEFT, STOP). Some children might be police officers who write tickets for violators.

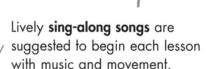

Music, Mazes & More CD-ROM

Music for Movement
ABC Rap (Track 2)
Wake Up Fingers (Track 4)
Hold Your Crayon (Track 8)
Slide Along (Track 10)

Optional Practice Pages
You may wish to use some of these practice pages in the writing center.

Mazes: Pages 1, 2, 5, 9
Picture/Letter Cards: Pages 13, 15
Letters: Pages 35, 36, 38

Lively **sing-along songs** are suggested to begin each lesson with music and movement.

Optional **practice pages** can be printed and placed in the writing center or sent home.

Center Time and **Play Time** activities use common classroom materials.

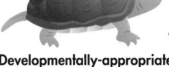

Stages of Early Writing Development

Young children develop as writers as they come to understand that writing is a powerful tool for communication. Between the ages of 2 and 6, children observe written messages in the world around them and experiment with making marks on paper. Through these explorations, they make important realizations about writing (see below).

Attention to the mechanics of handwriting (the specific skills necessary to hold a writing tool and form recognizable letters) should never overshadow the primary focus on the child's joy in writing messages to be read and appreciated by others. It is children's desire to write—their names, a note, or their stories—that fuels their passage through these five stages of development.

> Written messages have meaning.

> Drawing is different than writing.

> Written messages are created in lines.

> Letters are made from certain lines and shapes.

> There is a finite number of letters (26). Each has its own name and shape.

> Letters represent sounds and can be combined to form words.

Stage 1  Random Scribbling (ages 2–3)

Child makes random contact with the paper and exhibits little muscular control.

What to Teach: Encourage continued exploration of making marks with crayons and chalk. Allow time and materials for gross-motor and fine-motor development.

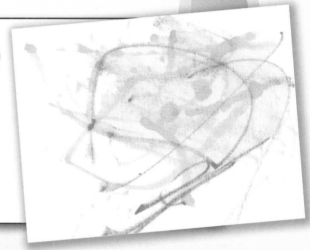

Stage 2 Controlled Scribbling (age 3)

Pretend writing is produced as child scribbles across paper in a linear fashion. Patterns may be repeated over and over. Shows increased muscular control.

What to Teach: Recognize the value of child's writing. Show how to secure paper with the helper hand. Blocks, puzzles, and self-care tasks allow development of the arms, hands, and wrists.

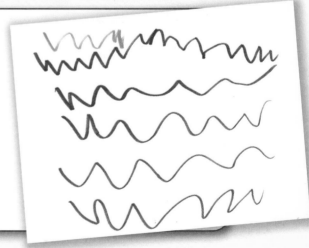

Stage 3  Mock Writing (ages 3–4)

Writing includes letter-like forms, often arranged in groups and word-like strings. Mock letters may include characteristics of familiar letters but may be misshapen, combined, reversed, or inverted. Children often write for a purpose, and a distinction is made between drawing and writing.

What to Teach: Letter recognition is important. Teach basic writing strokes and directions. Demonstrate a good writing grip as explained on page 13 of this Teacher Guide. Working on an easel, stringing beads, and doing simple crafts continue to develop fine-motor skills.

Stage 4  Writing Letters (ages 4–5)

Children name and write recognizable letters, although letters are frequently reversed. They write their names and other words that have personal meaning. These writers show an awareness that letters match sounds.

What to Teach: Demonstrate letter formation to avoid self-created and inefficient methods such as writing from bottom to top. Grouping letters that share common strokes will help develop correct motor patterns for writing letters. Forestall bad habits by continuing to encourage a good writing grip.

Stage 5 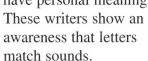 Writing Words (ages 5–6)

Using invented spelling, children group letters to write many words. Mature writing grip has developed. Children write letters, including lowercase letters, more smoothly and automatically. Dominant writing hand and use of helper hand (see page 13) are well-developed.

What to Teach: Assess that children have internalized correct, efficient motor pattern to write each letter. Monitor writing grip. Writing practice should be multisensory and include materials such as play dough, Touch and Trace Letter Cards, and Wikki Stix®.

Writing is a perceptual-motor skill that involves the whole child. Physical abilities, language skills, visual/perceptual factors, and cognitive development all play a part when a child puts crayon to paper. Few other classroom activities link the mind and the body so closely. Children need time to mature in all these ways before they are ready for formal writing instruction.

To prepare the whole child for writing, *On the Road to Writing and Reading* includes flexible teaching suggestions and materials to meet each child's developmental needs in seven key areas: Gross-Motor Skills, Fine-Motor Skills, Spatial Awareness, Print Awareness, Letter Recognition, Sound-Symbol Awareness, and Handwriting Skills.

Developing Gross-Motor Skills

Gross-motor skills depend on the development of the large muscles of the body, including those in the arms and legs. Large-muscle development is necessary for walking, lifting, jumping, and playing. Although gross-motor skills begin in infancy and precede fine-motor skills, it is important to provide opportunities for continued growth during the preschool years. A child's ability to coordinate his or her movements in the classroom, imitate the teacher's movements, and interact with the learning environment has a big impact on school success.

On the Road to Writing and Reading encourages gross-motor development through:

- Action songs found on the *Music, Mazes & More* CD-ROM

- Acting out the Stroke Story and sky-writing strokes and letters in the air while working with the Group Time Cards

- Fun activities such as jumping along a large line that has been chalked on the playground surface (see page 28)

Developing Fine-Motor Skills

Fine-motor skills relate to the development of small muscles found in the hands and other parts of the body. Skills include the ability to control the hands, fingers, and wrists, and the ability to carry out activities such as tearing, cutting, drawing, and writing. Because small muscles develop much later than large muscles, preschool children should never be expected to perform small-motor tasks that are beyond their abilities, such as writing perfectly formed letters on a line.

Experts agree that fine-motor skills are best encouraged by providing children with a variety of low-tech toys and materials for manipulation and exploration. The strength and control needed for writing are developed through play activities such as building with blocks, kneading and rolling dough, working puzzles, stringing beads, tracing, and cutting. Working on an easel or wall-mounted chalkboard is especially good for preparing the wrist and hand for writing.

On the Road to Writing and Reading encourages fine-motor development through:

- Finger warm-ups and fingerplays found on the *Music, Mazes & More* CD-ROM

- Mazes and tracing exercises found on the *Music, Mazes & More* CD-ROM

- Tactile/kinesthetic writing center materials such as Touch and Trace Letter Cards and Wikki Stix®.

- Fun activities such as cutting patterns (see page 92) and moving magnets through a maze (see page 108)

Developing Spatial Awareness

When children begin formal schooling, they enter a world of two-dimensional symbols such as letters and numerals. Prekindergarten teachers can help young children prepare for this new world by introducing important directional and spatial concepts using concrete, play-based experiences that are appropriate for young children. Top-to-bottom and left-to-right habits, so important for reading and writing, begin as children participate in body movement exercises and hands-on activities.

On the Road to Writing and Reading encourages the development of spatial awareness through:

- Action songs found on the *Music, Mazes & More* CD-ROM
- Colorful, traffic-sign directional cues on every Group Time Card
- Fun activities such as making a red ring to identify the right hand (see page 84)

Developing Print Awareness

Understanding concepts of print is a major step toward literacy for young children. Exposure to a wide variety of texts helps children realize that print is used for different purposes, that spoken language can be written down to carry a message, and that words are groups of letters separated by spaces on the page. In the prekindergarten environment, learning to write should be only part of a larger understanding of the power of print.

On the Road to Writing and Reading encourages the development of print awareness through:

- A shared/interactive writing suggestion for each Group Time
- Ideas for including purposeful writing during Play Time
- Fun activities such as making books about circles (see page 44)

Developing Letter Recognition

The ability to name each alphabet letter greatly simplifies the reading and writing task for young children. In fact, early letter recognition has proven to be a major predictor of later reading success. Children learn to recognize letters as they notice the visual attributes, including lines and curves, that make up their unique shapes. When children focus on learning to write letter shapes, their letter-specific knowledge and overall literacy development is enhanced.

On the Road to Writing and Reading encourages the development of letter recognition through:

- A primary focus on learning the basic strokes that make up letters

- Large, clear alphabet models for group work (Group Time Cards), individual support (Alphabet Cards), and home reinforcement (Home Alphabet Poster)

- Fun games such as "Going on a Letter Hunt" (see page 96)

Developing Sound-Symbol Awareness

Learning to write letters coincides with learning the sounds that letters make. For prekindergarteners, each skill enhances and simplifies the other. Children learn the alphabetic principle as they practice writing letters. Often, children are ready to use invented spelling to write words just about the time they have become comfortable with writing letter shapes. What a remarkable accomplishment!

On the Road to Writing and Reading encourages the development of sound-symbol awareness through:

- Interactive Stroke Stories about animal characters that represent letter sounds

- Word labels that contain key letters on every Group Time Card and Alphabet Card

- Fun activities such as moving like an animal after hearing a word that begins with the matching sound (see page 96)

Developing Handwriting Skills

Prekindergarten children are not ready for the demands of formal handwriting instruction. They should not be expected to write well-formed letters over and over, or to pay much attention to the size and proportion of letters and the spacing between them. However, young children should be offered a variety of appealing writing tools, especially unlined paper and crayons, which reward the writer with lots of space for writing and a wide, visible, textured line. Uppercase letters, with their straight lines and large curves, are easier for young children to write, and should be introduced before lowercase letters.

It is not appropriate to ask young children to sit still at desks or tables when they write, or to hold their paper "just so". However, prekindergarten is the right time to introduce hand-positioning habits that will help with handwriting for years to come. These include:

Establishing Hand Preference

To determine hand dominance, observe each child doing a variety of everyday tasks, such as using a hand puppet, cutting with scissors, throwing a ball, holding a spoon, and hammering a toy peg. Record hand preference for each activity. If a child is definitely left-handed, teach him or her to use that hand for holding the writing tool. If a child is truly ambidextrous, it is probably better to train the right hand.

Looking for the Helper Hand

When children write, ask, "Where is your helper hand? You need its help for writing!" The helper hand, or non-writing hand, should always be in sight on the tabletop, securing the paper and shifting it left-to-right as needed as children write. Teach children to get into the habit of looking for the helper hand.

Learning a Good Grip for Writing

It can be difficult to persuade a first- or second-grader to change the way he or she holds the writing tool, but prekindergarteners are usually receptive to learning a comfortable and efficient grip. During each writing lesson, model the three-finger hold, or tripod grip, shown below. Keep in mind that a mature writing grip develops over time and with lots of practice.

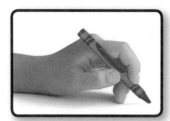

Left Hand **Right Hand**

Hold the crayon between the thumb, pointer, and middle fingers. The pointer rests on top. The end of the bent thumb is placed against the crayon to hold it high in the hand and near the knuckle.

Children who have difficulty with the traditional grip may prefer this alternative method of holding the crayon between the pointer and middle fingers.

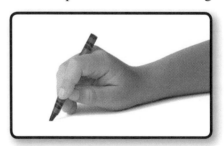

On the Road to Writing and Reading encourages handwriting development through:

* Flexible materials, such as Group Time Cards and Practice Pages, that teach letter formation when children are ready

* Hands-on, developmentally appropriate practice materials such as Letter Magnets and Touch and Trace Letter Cards

* Teacher Guide activities that help build a strong foundation for handwriting success

Lesson Overview

Group Time Days 1–2

During Group Time, children are introduced to a set of 2–3 letters that have similar shapes, strokes, and formations. Side A of each Group Time Card shows the featured stroke in each letter. Side B shows how to form the letters. During Group Time, children:

- Activate fine-motor skills and gross-motor skills by singing an action song from the *Music, Mazes & More* CD-ROM

- Listen to a Stroke Story that explains the featured stroke, and participate actively by moving their bodies

- Use sky-writing to write each stroke and letter in the air

- Identify the featured letters on the Alphabet Road

- Write a message using shared/interactive writing

Meet individual needs by:

- Using only the uppercase Group Time Cards. Proficiency in writing the uppercase letters will help prepare children to write lowercase letters in kindergarten.

- Using only Side A of the Group Time Cards. Children who are not ready to learn the detailed formation of each letter can instead focus on the basic strokes and directions important for writing.

- Inviting children to individually touch and trace strokes and letters on the Group Time Card instead of sky-writing. For some children, touching the card may be a simpler and more direct way to experience the lesson.

- Stretching out and repeating Group Time activities over a week or longer. A brief Group Time may precede plenty of writing center time and other hands-on writing practice activities during each day of focus on the targeted letters.

Center Time Days 3–5

During Center Time, children engage in one or more multisensory practice activities using a variety of hands-on materials. Specific practice activities may be guided by the teacher, or a variety of materials may be offered in the writing center for ongoing practice. High quality writing practice activities encourage children to *look* closely at strokes and letters, to *say* stroke names and letter names out loud, and to use the hands to *touch*, trace, and manipulate letter shapes.

Meet individual needs by:

- Deciding whether or not to use Practice Page exercises from the *Music, Mazes & More* CD-ROM. These pages may be offered to introduce children to crayon-and-paper practice, or may be skipped in favor of more play-based practice options.

- Encouraging children to practice writing strokes and shapes and to draw pictures as well as writing letters and words.

- Consistently offering practice materials that invite free exploration of letter shapes (such as Letter Magnets) as well as more structured options that ask children to form letters (such as Practice Pages).

- Continuing to offer Center Time practice activities throughout the school year for letters that have been introduced.

Play Time Days 3–5

During Play Time, children are encouraged to use writing for authentic purposes during free play and dramatic play times. Play scenarios related to the Stroke Stories and Group Time Card illustrations are suggested. Children benefit from writing their own lists, signs, labels, etc., as they play as well as from using print material and teacher-prepared props that include text.

Meet individual needs by:

- Accepting and valuing children's play writing, even if it consists of scribbling.

- Providing enough materials so that everyone has a chance to write.

- Offering Play Time writing experiences more often early in the year so that children become more comfortable with writing.

Why aren't letters presented in alphabetical order?

On the Road to Writing and Reading presents letters in order of handwriting difficulty. Although **A** is the first letter of the alphabet, it contains two slant strokes, which present the greatest challenge for young children to write. Straight line letters such as **L, T,** and **E** are the easiest to write, so they come first. This sequence is developmentally appropriate and gives young children the best path for success with writing letters.

Why are letters presented in groups?

The Group Time Cards present sets of 2–3 letters that share common strokes, formation patterns, and visual attributes. Grouping similar letters helps young children by taking some of the mystery out of the writing task. It shows that there are logical patterns to the business of writing letters.

When a child sees an individual letter, such as **E**, and attempts to write it, he or she may think, "Let me look at this letter and try to copy its shape." In many cases, this practice results in self-invented and inefficient methods for writing letters, such as writing the vertical line in **E** from bottom-to-top or writing the horizontal lines in **E** from right-to-left. By presenting **E** with its stroke cousins **F** and **H** (both of which contain vertical and horizontal lines), children see the patterns and learn to write letters correctly and efficiently.

The fact that letters are presented in groups in no way suggests an accelerated pace for learning to write letters. Young children need ample time to learn and practice each letter in a variety of ways.

Why are both uppercase and lowercase letters included?

All 52 letterforms of the uppercase and lowercase alphabet and the numerals 1–10 are included to give prekindergarten teachers multiple options for teaching children to recognize and write letters. Uppercase letters, with their straight lines and large curves, should be taught first. Lowercase letters include retraced lines and tighter curves that are more difficult for children to write. Some children may not be ready for lowercase letters until kindergarten.

What is the purpose of the yellow traffic sign directions?

The yellow traffic signs shown on each Group Time Card provide a constant reminder that readers and writers move across the page from top-to-bottom and from left-to-right. In many cases, the arrows will help children write the featured strokes and letters correctly.

Why are there green dots on the letters?

A green dot shows the correct starting point for each letter. Learning the starting position for letters gets children going in the right direction and can eliminate reversed letters. Teachers can encourage this habit by using a green pen to make a dot on children's papers when they model letter formation.

How do music and movement help children write?

Taking time to move and stretch the hands and body can be a signal for children that writing time is about to begin. Choose one of the action songs from the *Music, Mazes & More* CD-ROM to begin Group Time. Be sure to frequently include songs with finger motions that strengthen the hands and develop fine-motor skills. Warm up children's fingers with these options:

- Sing "Wake Up Fingers," "Thumbs Up," or "Thumbkin," from the *Music, Mazes & More* CD-ROM
- Choose another familiar action song or favorite fingerplay
- Ask children to name and wiggle each finger before touching it to the palm: thumb, pointer, middle, ring, pinky
- Alternately stretch the fingers wide and squeeze them into fists
- Identify and "greet" the dominant (writing) hand, the helper hand, and the three fingers children use to hold their crayons (the thumb, pointer, and middle finger of the dominant hand)

What is sky-writing?

Sky-writing is a technique that allows children to use their large muscles to practice the motor patterns used to form strokes and letters. To sky-write, hold up the index and middle fingers of the writing hand and raise the whole arm.

Children should follow the teacher in forming the featured strokes and letters at a large size in the air. As they sky-write, children should repeat the name of each stroke after the teacher. The teacher should either reverse her motions or turn her back so that it is not necessary for children to mirror the teacher's actions. "Sky-Writing," found on the *Music, Mazes & More* CD-ROM, is a fun way to teach the technique.

What is shared/interactive writing and why is it important?

Shared/interactive writing occurs when teachers and children compose a message together. In *On the Road to Writing and Reading*, shared/interactive writing offers a way for children to put their new writing skills to work along with their broader literacy knowledge. Teachers and children can agree on a message to write on chart paper that relates to the Group Time lesson. Children should be encouraged to match letters and sounds as the teacher writes and to recognize the target letters in the message. Finally, teachers can point out that letters combine to make words and that there is less space between letters than between words.

What kinds of practice are recommended?

Keep writing practice fun and stimulating by offering a variety of activities in this Teacher Guide. The following items are included in the *On the Road to Writing and Reading* kit:

Group Time Cards: Children can trace strokes and letters on these laminated cards with wax crayons or dry-erase markers. They can use Wikki Stix, play dough, clay, or other wipe-away materials to build letters right on the card models. Cards can be displayed around the room to provide writing models.

Alphabet Cards: These laminated cards work well in the writing center or for tabletop work. Directional arrows guide letter formation as children work with the cards at close range. Children can trace letters on the cards with wax crayons or dry-erase markers. They can use Wikki Stix, play dough, clay or other wipe-away materials to build letters right on the card models. Children can sort the letters by shapes or sounds. They can sequence cards to spell and write words.

Wikki Stix®: Wax-coated strings may be bent, curved, and shaped to form lines, letters, and words. Wikki Stix stick to any non-porous surface and are easily removed. Children can use them to "write" on laminated cards, paper, tabletops, windows, and walls. Different colored Wikki Stix may be used to show different kinds of lines within letters.

Touch and Trace Letter Cards: Children put the pointer finger of the writing hand into the textured groove. They trace the letter, beginning at the arrow that shows the starting point, reinforcing the correct motor pathway for forming each letter. An auditory component may be added as children say the names of each line in the letter. Cards may also be used to make letter rubbings for more tracing practice.

Magnetic Letters and Board: These foam magnets match *Zaner-Bloser* letters. Using letter magnets gives children a chance to pick up letter shapes, touch their lines and curves, and examine them from all angles. Magnets may be sorted and sequenced according to letter shapes and sounds. A dry-erase marker may also be used on the magnetic board.

Optional Practice Pages: These pages may be printed from the *Music, Mazes & More* CD-ROM and distributed for guided whole-group practice, writing center practice, or take-home practice. Pages include prewriting practice in completing mazes, writing lines, and recognizing letters, as well as letter and numeral writing practice. Completed pages may be assembled into alphabet books. Practice pages may be used as a culminating or assessment activity after children have engaged in many kinds of hands-on practice.

How much writing practice do young children need?

Be careful not to overdo writing practice. It is not appropriate to ask young children to fill several lines or a page by writing a letter over and over. Remember that practice makes permanent. If a child practices an incorrect formation, it can become a habit. The quality of practice is more important than quantity. Multisensory practice activities should encourage children to write a letter correctly two to four times.

What is multisensory practice?

Multisensory practice activities allow children to *see* a good model of the letter to be written, *say* or hear the names of the lines it contains, and *touch*, trace, or manipulate the letter shape in some way. This type of visual, auditory, and tactile/kinesthetic practice engages children with different learning styles and developmental abilities.

How many letters should children practice at a time?

Allow children time to practice each letter by itself, with other similar letters, and in words. Children's writing will become smoother and more automatic as they encounter letters over many days and weeks.

What about when children write at home?

Confusion can arise when parents teach children to write letters one way at home and teachers present a different model at school. This confusion can be eliminated by distributing the *On the Road to Writing and Reading* Home Poster to each family. The poster contains models for a good writing grip, tips for writing together at home, and an alphabet poster to display on the refrigerator. Ask parents to refer to the directional arrows on the poster when they are showing children how to write letters at home.

What is a writing center and what supplies should it contain?

A writing center is a special area of the classroom devoted to writing. While it may sometimes contain supplies and directions for a specific practice activity, its main purpose is to provide materials and inspiration for young writers who are eager to express themselves. The writing center may be a single large table or several smaller tables or desks with nearby shelves to hold supplies. A bulletin board provides a place to publish writing and shoeboxes or folders might serve as individual mailboxes so that children can communicate through writing. The writing center should contain many kinds of supplies for writing, including:

- unlined and lined paper and stationery of all sizes and shapes
- crayons, markers, and chalk
- letter formation models (such as Alphabet Cards) and models of important names and words children will want to write
- scissors, tape, stapler, hole punch, yarn, and other book-making supplies
- junk mail, envelopes, notebooks, and other real-world writing supplies
- a chalkboard or dry-erase board

Why is it important to write during Play Time?

When children engage in dramatic play and free play, they often act out roles of adults and older children. Through their play behaviors, they "reach" for the next stages of maturity. When writing is incorporated into this type of play, children learn to emulate and value writing as an important and desirable part of the world around them. They understand common purposes of writing and expand their own reasons to write. In addition, Play Time writing provides another way to practice children's new writing skills.

What if children's Play Time writing is messy or incorrect?

That's okay. This is not the time to teach letter formation or to actively guide children's writing. Instead, it is a chance for children to write for authentic purposes, using whatever written marks are comfortable for them at their stage of development. Because they often witness adults quickly writing a check or a note, children may speed up their writing during play, making it more scribbled and less legible. This is just the child's way of saying, "Someday I will be a proficient and important writer, too."

Should every child write during Play Time?

Ideally, every child will engage in literacy behaviors, including writing, during Play Time. Some children may be more inclined to write than others. Plenty of materials should be provided to give everyone a chance. Teachers should suggest new ways to incorporate writing that may not be obvious to children. Carpenters and construction workers can jot down measurements, airplane pilots can note weather conditions, and athletes can create plays, rosters, or new team names.

What materials facilitate Play Time writing?

Provide real-world writing materials including notepads, stationery, junk mail, labels, price tags, sign-making supplies, menus and recipe books, catalogs, scoreboards, and sticky notes. Teachers may also introduce signs, labels, and other text-based materials they have prepared as good models for writing. Children will find ways to use them all.

Objectives
- Recognize pull down lines and slide lines
- Write pull down lines from top to bottom
- Write slide lines from left to right
- Listen to stories
- Develop oral language and writing skills

Kit Materials
- Group Time Card 1
- *Music, Mazes & More* CD-ROM
- Wikki Stix®

Classroom Materials
- Blank paper, crayons
- Pretend fire station materials
- Stickers or bingo paint markers
- Sidewalk chalk or masking tape
- Green construction paper, tape

Stroke Focus

Pull down.

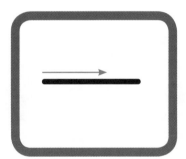

Slide.

Teacher Tips
The vertical line, or pull down line, is developmentally the simplest to write. The horizontal line, or slide line, comes next. Although the motions used to write these lines will be easy for most children, the task of controlling the crayon in order to write distinct, regular lines will be a challenge for many preschoolers. These skills develop with time and practice. Don't be concerned if children's lines seem too long. In time, they will learn to stop the crayon more deliberately. Once children are used to the feel of pull down and slide lines, encourage them to combine the two to draw cross shapes, squares, and rectangles.

Stroke Story

Children act out motions shown in red.

It's a busy day at the fire station. The animal firefighters use the fire pole to go quickly from the top floor to the bottom floor. *(Hold up nondominant forearm to represent pole.)* Snake goes down the pole, from top to bottom. *(Slither writing hand down pole.)* Grasshopper hops down. *(Hop hand down pole.)* Hawk swoops down. *(Dive hand down along pole.)* Last comes big, heavy Bear. *(Begin to move fist down pole.)* Get out of the way, smaller firefighters! You don't want Bear to land on you! *(Wiggle fingers away from bottom of pole.)* Plop! Bear is down. *(Plop fist to bottom of pole.)* They're off to fight the fire!

Music, Mazes & More CD-ROM

Music for Movement
Wake Up Fingers (Track 4)
My Two Hands (Track 7)
I Pull Down (Track 9)

Optional Practice Pages
You may wish to use some of these practice pages in the writing center.

Basic Strokes: Pages 19, 20

22

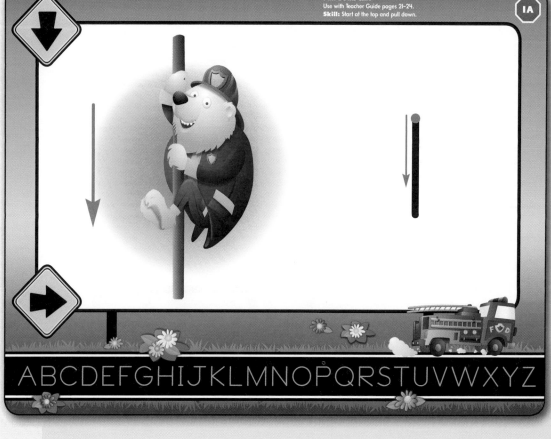

Pull Down Line
Use with Teacher Guide pages 21–24.
Skill: Start at the top and pull down.

1A

ABCDEFGHIJKLMNOPQRSTUVWXYZ

1. Group Time Days 1–2

*Gather children together for group time. Use the **Group Time** information on pages 16–17 and the notes below.*

Group Time Card 1A

1. Warm up with a song. Choose one listed at left.
2. Tell the Stroke Story at left.
3. Start at the green dot. Trace the line from top to bottom. Say "pull down."
4. Sky-write the line several times. Say "pull down."

2. Center Time Days 3–5

*Choose multisensory activities for writing practice from the **Center Time** information on pages 18–19 or the activity below.*

Fire Pole Show children how to use one Wikki Stix piece to make a long fire pole from the top to the bottom of a sheet of blank paper. Crayon a green dot at the top and a pink arrow going down beside. Use another Wikki Stix piece to form a small human or animal figure. Move the figure down the pole from top to bottom, saying "pull down."

3. Play Time Days 3–5

*Use the **Play Time** information on page 20 and the idea below to introduce purposeful writing into children's dramatic play.*

Fire Station Provide materials to make badges, hats, and signs. Notepads may be used to write down addresses where people need help. Safety rules and fire fighting instructions might be posted. Written awards may be given to brave fire fighters.

Slide Line
Use with Teacher Guide pages 21–24.
Skill: Slide from left to right.

IB

ABCDEFGHIJKLMNOPQRSTUVWXYZ

Copyright © Zaner-Bloser, Inc.

Stroke Story

Children act out motions shown in red.

Let's play with a wagon. Hop in the back. (Children sit on the floor, facing right.) Cat will slide us along. The wagon is going slowly. (Scoot slowly to the right.) No, that's too fast! (Scoot quickly.) Now the ride is smooth. That's better. (Scoot smoothly.) Cat, why is the ride getting jerky now? (Scoot, stop, scoot, stop.) I don't think you can walk very well in those dress-up shoes. Oh, no, you're going to tip the wagon! (Fall over on the floor.) Let's get back in the wagon and slide again.

1. Group Time Days 1–2

*Gather children together for group time. Use the **Group Time** information on pages 16–17 and the notes below.*

Group Time Card IB

1. Warm up with a song. Choose one listed at right.
2. Tell the Stroke Story at right.
3. Start at the green dot. Trace the line from left to right. Say "slide."
4. Sky-write the line several times. Say "slide."

2. Center Time Days 3–5

*Choose multisensory activities for writing practice from the **Center Time** information on pages 18–19 or the activity below.*

Checkerboard Provide large, blank drawing paper. Show how to write pull down lines that start at the top. Show how to write slide lines that start at the left. This will form a checkerboard pattern. Point out that children have made squares. Children can put stickers in some of the squares. Or provide bingo paint markers so they can paint dots in the squares.

3. Play Time Days 3–5

*Use the **Play Time** information on page 20 and the idea below to introduce purposeful writing into children's dramatic play.*

Sidewalk Play on an outdoor sidewalk or a pretend sidewalk you have made with masking tape on the floor. Provide materials for making street signs, lemonade stands, and house and building numbers. Sidewalk chalk (outdoors) or chart paper and markers (indoors) may be used to draw hopscotch or other games.

Music, Mazes & More
CD-ROM

Music for Movement
Top to Bottom (Track 3)
Thumbkin (Track 6)
Sing Along (Track 10)

Optional Practice Pages
You may wish to use some of these practice pages in the writing center.

Mazes: Pages 1, 2, 5, 9
Basic Strokes: Pages 21, 22

Fun With Fundamentals

See pages 10–13 for more information about the development of these essential prewriting skills.

Developing Gross-Motor Skills

Show children safe and fun ways to move from top to bottom and from left to right. For top-to-bottom, they might go down a pole on the playground or jump down from a low step or platform. For left-to-right, show how to sashay-step by bringing the feet together, swinging the right foot out to the side, then bringing the feet together again.

Developing Fine-Motor Skills

Children build hand skills as they stack, sort, place, and manipulate blocks, beads, counters, puzzle pieces, and other small items. These actions help children master the dual functions of the hand—using the pointer finger and thumb for precision movements and the ring and pinky fingers for stabilizing.

Developing Spatial Awareness

Cut a green construction paper circle and place a loop of tape on the back. Go on a walk around the room, pointing out pull down lines (the leg of a chair, the side of a doorway, the side of a poster) and slide lines (lines on a calendar, a table edge, the window sill). For each, invite a volunteer to stick the green dot at the top (for pull down lines) or at the left (for slide lines).

Developing Print Awareness

Distribute paper and crayons to children. As you read the following story aloud, ask children to make horizontal (slide) lines or vertical (pull down) lines. Model the lines on chart paper. Emphasize beginning at the top of the paper and starting each line at the left edge. See the sample at right.

1. Let's take a walk. We'll use slide lines to show our walk. (Draw slide lines.)

2. Oh, it's raining. What kind of lines will show the rain? (Draw pull down lines.)

3. Still raining! (pull down lines)

4. It's fun to slide in the puddle. Let's make long slide lines! (slide lines)

5. Here's the neighbor's picket fence. Which lines show a fence? (pull down lines)

6. Let's run all the way home. (slide lines)

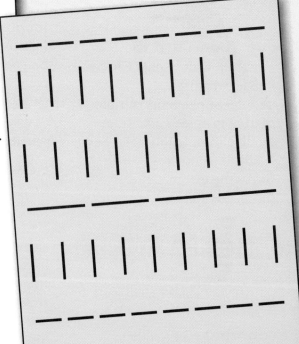

Objectives
- Recognize circle lines
- Write circle back lines
- Write circle forward lines
- Listen to stories
- Develop oral language and writing skills

Kit Materials
- Group Time Card 2
- *Music, Mazes & More* CD-ROM
- Wikki Stix®

Classroom Materials
- Blank paper, crayons, glue, yarn
- Pretend bakery supplies
- Cardstock for making stencils
- Sidewalk chalk or masking tape
- Pretend repair shop supplies
- Toy cars
- Pipe cleaners

Stroke Focus

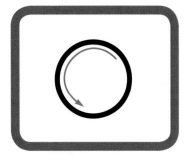

Circle back.

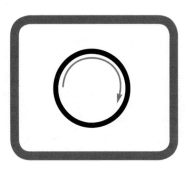

Circle forward.

Teacher Tips

Circles and curves are the next shapes to emerge in children's drawing and writing. Demonstrate that circles can go around in two directions, but don't be concerned if children initially confuse the "backward" and "forward" distinctions taught in this lesson. You may wish to point out that circle forward lines circle to the right and that circle back lines circle to the left.

Starting and stopping circles at the same spot can be challenging for preschoolers. Don't expect perfect circles, but do discourage writing circles with short, choppy lines. Tactile experiences—such as writing circles in a tray of sand or forming circles from ropes of play dough—will help children form smooth circles.

Stroke Story

Children act out motions shown in red.

Let's help Chicken make cookies. Get a big bowl (position pretend bowl in lap; secure with non-writing hand) and a big spoon (hold pretend spoon with writing hand). Pour in some milk and stir. (Pour, then stir in counterclockwise motion.) Sprinkle in flour and seeds. (Sprinkle, then stir in counterclockwise motion.) Put in a cup of corn. (Dump cup; stir.) Put in TWO cups of wiggly worms. Yum! Stir it all together. (Stir in counterclockwise motion.) Now put the cookies in the oven. Chicken cookies are my favorite!

Music, Mazes & More CD-ROM

Music for Movement
Sky-Writing (Track 1)
Wake Up Fingers (Track 4)
Circle Song (Track 11)

Optional Practice Pages
You may wish to use some of these practice pages in the writing center.

Basic Strokes: Pages 23, 24

Circle Back Line
Use with Teacher Guide pages 25–28.
Skill: Beginning at the 1:00 position, circle back.

2A

COOKIES

ABCDEFGHIJKLMNOPQRSTUVWXYZ

1 Group Time Days 1–2

Gather children together for group time. Use the **Group Time** information on pages 16–17 and the notes below.

Group Time Card 2A
1. Warm up with a song. Choose one listed at left.
2. Tell the Stroke Story at left.
3. Start at the green dot. Trace the line with a counterclockwise motion. Say "circle back."
4. Sky-write the line several times. Extend writing hand to a 1:00 position to begin. Say "circle back."

2 Center Time Days 3–5

Choose multisensory activities for writing practice from the **Center Time** information on pages 18–19 or the activity below.

Chicken's Cookie For each child, prepare a sheet of paper with a green dot at the 1:00 position and a length of yarn. Show how to apply glue to the paper in a large backward circle, beginning and ending at the green dot. Using the same motion, press the yarn into the glue to make a circle. This is Chicken's cookie. Color it and draw corn, worms, and other ingredients inside. Children can trace the yarn with the pointer finger of the writing hand, beginning at the green dot and saying "circle back."

3 Play Time Days 3–5

Use the **Play Time** information on page 20 and the idea below to introduce purposeful writing into children's dramatic play.

Bakery Organize a pretend bakery with bakers, clerks, and delivery workers. Provide play dough, bowls, utensils, trays, hot pads, and a display. Encourage writing by supplying recipe cards, sign making materials, and blank labels and price tags.

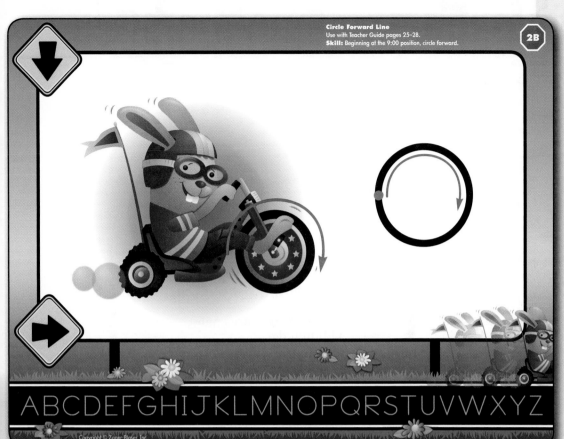

Circle Forward Line
Use with Teacher Guide pages 25–28.
Skill: Beginning at the 9:00 position, circle forward.

2B

ABCDEFGHIJKLMNOPQRSTUVWXYZ

Stroke Story

Children act out motions shown in red.

Rabbit has a new bike, but she is not sure how to ride it. She puts her feet on the pedals. (Lie on back with feet in the air.) She pushes with one foot and the wheel moves a little bit. (Push out with one foot.) She pushes the other pedal. (Push with other foot.) The bike hasn't moved very far. Rabbit tries pedaling with one foot and then the other to make a circle. (Pedal feet in air in complete circle.) It works! The pedals make the wheel turn in a fast circle. The bike zooms along!

1. Group Time Days 1–2

*Gather children together for group time. Use the **Group Time** information on pages 16–17 and the notes below.*

Group Time Card 2B

1. Warm up with a song. Choose one listed at right.
2. Tell the Stroke Story at right.
3. Start at the green dot. Trace the line in a clockwise motion. Say "circle forward."
4. Sky-write the line several times. Extend writing hand to a 9:00 position to begin. Say "circle forward."

2. Center Time Days 3–5

*Choose multisensory activities for writing practice from the **Center Time** information on pages 18–19 or the activity below.*

Circle Stories Cut several 3–5" circles from cardstock. On each, draw a green dot at the 9:00 position. Provide these stencils, as well as large, blank drawing paper and crayons. Show how to trace the stencils in a clockwise motion, beginning and ending at the green dot. Demonstrate how to secure the stencil with the helper hand. Completed circles can be incorporated into crayon drawings of vehicles, pizzas, balls, etc.

3. Play Time Days 3–5

*Use the **Play Time** information on page 20 and the idea below to introduce purposeful writing into children's dramatic play.*

Repair Shop Establish a vehicle repair shop outdoors. Customers may bring in bikes, cars, and wagons for inspection and repair. Encourage writing by providing materials to make job orders, license plates, driver's licenses, signs, invoices.

Music, Mazes & More CD-ROM

Music for Movement
Thumbs Up (Track 5)
Hold Your Crayon (Track 8)
Circle Song (Track 11)

Optional Practice Pages
You may wish to use some of these practice pages in the writing center.

Mazes: Pages 3, 7, 11
Basic Strokes: Pages 25, 26

Fun With Fundamentals

See pages 10–13 for more information about the development of these essential prewriting skills.

Developing Gross-Motor Skills

Make two large circles on the playground surface with sidewalk chalk or on the floor with masking tape. Draw or tape a green beginning dot at the 1:00 position (for the circle back line) and at the 9:00 position (for the circle forward line). Invite children to jump, run, skip, or ride vehicles along the lines, beginning at the green dots.

Developing Fine-Motor Skills

Completing mazes helps children develop hand control and motor planning. Print and laminate several of the mazes from the *Music, Mazes & More* CD-ROM. Provide toy cars so that children can drive them along the maze path.

Developing Spatial Awareness

Play a game of "Simon Says" using directional words. Commands might include: touch the top of your head, sit down on the floor, raise the hand you use for writing, put your left hand on your belly, circle your arms around.

Developing Print Awareness

Provide a pipe cleaner for each child to bend into the shape of a magnifying glass. Then go on a walk around the classroom, asking children to look through their magnifying glasses to spy circles in letters they find on signs, posters, charts, books, etc.

Objectives
- Recognize slant lines
- Write slanted lines
- Listen to stories
- Develop oral language and writing skills

Kit Materials
- Group Time Card 3
- *Music, Mazes & More* CD-ROM
- Wikki Stix®

Classroom Materials
- Large craft stick for each child
- Drawing paper, crayons
- Construction paper rectangles
- Glue
- Pretend construction site materials
- Several gallon-sized zip-top bags
- Hair gel
- Butcher paper, markers, blocks
- Eyedroppers, bowls, coffee filters
- Flashlight

Stroke Focus

Slant up.

Slant right.

Slant left.

Teacher Tips

Slant lines are the most difficult kinds of lines for children to write. Preschoolers are often unsure of how to begin slant lines, and where to aim them. There is a perceptual challenge in forming a clear mental image of a slant line before attempting to write it.

Spend time discussing what a slant line, or "leaning line," is. Look for examples of slant lines all around. Practice beginning at one spot and slanting out in different directions. Above all, encourage children's efforts to understand and write slant lines. Mastery will come with time and practice.

Stroke Story

Children act out motions shown in red. Make "ladders" by drawing short horizontal lines on large craft sticks. Give one to each child.

The dogs on the construction crew always take a ladder when they work on a tall building. The ladder won't work when it goes across. (Hold stick horizontally.) It won't work when it stands straight up. (Hold stick vertically.) It only works when it tips, or slants, up to the roof. (Slant ladder up to the right.) When the dogs are ready to come down, they slant the ladder down to the ground. (Slant stick down to the right.)

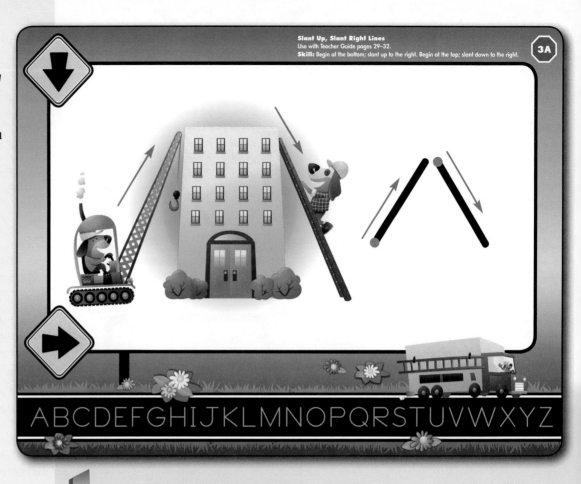

Slant Up, Slant Right Lines
Use with Teacher Guide pages 29–32.
Skill: Begin at the bottom; slant up to the right. Begin at the top; slant down to the right.

3A

ABCDEFGHIJKLMNOPQRSTUVWXYZ

Music, Mazes & More CD-ROM

Music for Movement
Sky-Writing (Track 1)
Thumbkin (Track 6)
Slant Dance (Track 12)

Optional Practice Pages
You may wish to use some of these practice pages in the writing center.

Basic Strokes: Pages 27, 28

30

Group Time Days 1–2

*Gather children together for group time. Use the **Group Time** information on pages 16–17 and the notes below.*

Group Time Card 3A
1. Warm up with a song. Choose one listed at left.
2. Tell the Stroke Story at left.
3. Start at the green dot. Trace the first line from bottom to top. Say "slant up." Trace the second line down to the right. Say "slant right."
4. Sky-write the lines several times. Say "slant up" or "slant right."

Center Time Days 3–5

*Choose multisensory activities for writing practice from the **Center Time** information on pages 18–19 or the activity below.*

Ladders Use "ladder" craft sticks from the Group Time story. Provide blank drawing paper, crayons, glue, and rectangles cut from construction paper. Show how to glue a rectangle to the paper for a building. Pull down lines and slide lines may be used to crayon doors and windows. Then use the craft stick as a stencil to write slant lines up to the top of the building on the left side and down to the ground on the right side.

Play Time Days 3–5

*Use the **Play Time** information on page 20 and the idea below to introduce purposeful writing into children's dramatic play.*

Construction Site Provide hats, large blocks or cardboard boxes, orange cones, measuring tapes, and tools. Encourage writing by supplying paper for noting measurements, drawing building plans, and making safety signs and building labels.

Slant Left Line
Use with Teacher Guide pages 29–32.
Skill: Begin at the top; slant down to the left.

3B

ABCDEFGHIJKLMNOPQRSTUVWXYZ

Copyright © Zaner-Bloser, Inc.

Stroke Story

Children act out motions shown in red.

Raccoon loves to go down the slide. The sliding board slants down to the ground. (Make a slide by sitting on the floor, facing left, with knees together and shins slanted. Use fist of writing hand to be the raccoon going down the slide.) Raccoon's little brother has never gone down the slide before. "Don't be scared," said Raccoon. "Let's go down together." The two go up together and zoom down. (Use two fists to go down the "slide.")

1. Group Time Days 1–2

Gather children together for group time. Use the Group Time information on pages 16–17 and the notes below.

Group Time Card 3B

1. Warm up with a song. Choose one listed at right.
2. Tell the Stroke Story at right.
3. Start at the green dot. Trace the line down to the left. Say "slant left."
4. Sky-write the line several times. Say "slant left."

2. Center Time Days 3–5

Choose multisensory activities for writing practice from the Center Time information on pages 18–19 or the activity below.

Gel Writing Squeeze a thick layer of hair gel or another gel-like substance, such as dish soap, into several gallon-sized zip-top bags. Seal the bags tight and flatten them. Show how to write slant lines by placing the pointer finger of the writing hand at one corner of the bag and tracing to the opposite corner. Smooth out the gel to "erase." The helper hand should secure the bag.

3. Play Time Days 3–5

Use the Play Time information on page 20 and the idea below to introduce purposeful writing into children's dramatic play.

Block Playground Spread butcher paper on the floor. Invite children to build a park from blocks on the paper. They might build sliding boards and other play equipment as well as benches, sports fields, and shelter houses. Provide crayons and markers so children can draw roads, paths, and lakes, and write signs.

Music, Mazes & More CD-ROM

Music for Movement
My Two Hands (Track 7)
Hold Your Crayon (Track 8)
Slant Dance (Track 12)

Optional Practice Pages
You may wish to use some of these practice pages in the writing center.

Mazes: Pages 4, 8
Basic Strokes: Pages 29, 30

Fun With Fundamentals

See pages 10–13 for more information about the development of these essential prewriting skills.

Developing Gross-Motor Skills

Say, "I am thinking of a kind of line—pull down, slide, circle, or slant." Then play some fun music for movement. Stop the music and tell children to form any of the four kinds of lines with their bodies. They might put arms straight in the air for a pull down line, put legs together on the floor for a slide line, curl into a ball for a circle line, or lean against the wall for a slant line. After children have posed, announce which kind of line you were thinking of. One child who chose to mimic that type of line can be "it"—the one who next thinks of a kind of line and stops the music.

Developing Fine-Motor Skills

Supply eye droppers, several bowls of water, and several empty bowls. Show how to use the eye dropper to transfer water to an empty bowl. Challenge children to release a certain number of water drops at a time.

You can also have children release drops of colored water onto clean coffee filters to make designs.

Developing Spatial Awareness

On the chalkboard or marker board, draw a large green dot. Write **L** a short distance to the left of the dot and **R** a short distance to the right of the dot. Help children understand that **L** means "left" and **R** means "right". Give a flashlight to a volunteer and turn off the lights. Ask the volunteer to point the flashlight beam at the dot and slant it in the direction you say—slant up to the right, slant down to the right, or slant down to the left. Repeat with additional volunteers.

Developing Print Awareness

Use the "ladder" craft sticks prepared for the Group Time story. Take a walk around the classroom so that children can match the angle of their craft sticks to slant lines they find on signs, posters, and books.

Featured Letters

Objectives
- Recognize the letters **L, T, I**
- Write pull down lines from top to bottom
- Write the letters **L, T, I**
- Listen to a story
- Develop oral language and writing skills

Kit Materials
- Group Time Card 4
- *Music, Mazes & More* CD-ROM
- Alphabet Cards **L, T, I**
- Magnetic Letters and Board
- Touch and Trace Letter Cards **L, T, I**
- Wikki Stix®

Classroom Materials
- Cup
- Hole punch
- Pipe cleaner
- String or yarn
- Blank paper and crayons
- Magnifying glass, notebook, crayons for nature walk
- Chalkboard, chalk, paintbrush
- Old newspapers and magazines
- Scissors, glue

Stroke Focus

Pull down.

Letter Focus

1. Pull down.
   Slide.

1. Pull down.
2. Slide.

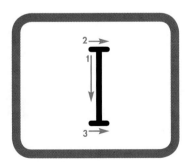

1. Pull down.
2. Slide.
3. Slide.

Teacher Tips

These letters begin by pulling down. Slide lines are then added. Practicing the individual lines, as well as combining them to draw squares and rectangles, will help prepare children to write **L**, **T**, and **I**.

Most preschoolers will find it challenging to join vertical and horizontal lines precisely. Don't be concerned if **T**'s "hat" doesn't sit perfectly or if **I**'s slide lines seem too long. Concentrating on directionality (top-to-bottom, left-to-right) and on the correct starting point for each letter will give children a solid foundation for future writing success.

Stroke Story

Children act out motions shown in red. Prepare a basket prop by punching two holes in a paper cup, threading a pipe cleaner handle through, and tying the handle to a piece of string or yarn.

Tiger has been playing in the tree house all morning. He has looked at many things high in the tree. Now he wants to explore on the ground. How will he get his exploring things down? He'll have to send them down in the basket. First he puts in some leaves. (A volunteer puts pretend leaves in the basket and lowers the basket downward.) The leaves go down and dump onto the ground. (Put three fingers of the writing hand in the air—pointer, thumb, and middle—and pull down, following the motion of the basket prop.)

(Repeat as three more volunteers put pretend objects in the basket and lower them as children sky-write the motion: juice box, notebook and crayon, magnifying glass.)

When all his things are down, Tiger carefully climbs down the ladder. (Use hands and feet to climb down a pretend ladder.) He is ready for more exploring.

Learn L, T, I
Use with Teacher Guide pages 33–36.
Skill: These letters have a pull down line.

4A

ABCDEFGHI JKLMNOPQRSTUVWXYZ

Group Time Days 1–2

*Gather children together for group time. Use the **Group Time** information on pages 16–17 and the notes below.*

Group Time Card 4A

1. Warm up with a song. Choose one listed at right.
2. Tell the Stroke Story.
3. Trace the arrow beside the basket from top to bottom. Say "pull down."
4. Sing "ABC Rap." Point to the target letters in yellow on the Alphabet Road.
5. Sky-write pull down lines in **L, T, I**. For each, say "pull down."

Group Time Card 4B

1. Warm up with a song. Choose one listed at right.
2. Sing "ABC Rap." Point to the letters on the Alphabet Road. Clap when you come to **L, T,** and **I**.

3. Talk about the letter shapes. The slide lines are at the bottom (**L**), at the top (**T**) or both (**I**). Who has these letters in his or her name? Can these letters be found in the room? Read the word for each letter. Find the letter in the word.
4. Sky-write each letter several times, beginning at the green dot and following the arrows. Say the name of each line aloud.
5. Write an uppercase message, such as I LIKE YOUR TREE, TIGER, using shared or interactive writing. Read the message together, pointing to letters, words, and spaces.

34

Write L, T, I
Use with Teacher Guide pages 33–36.
Skill: Begin these letters by pulling down.

4B

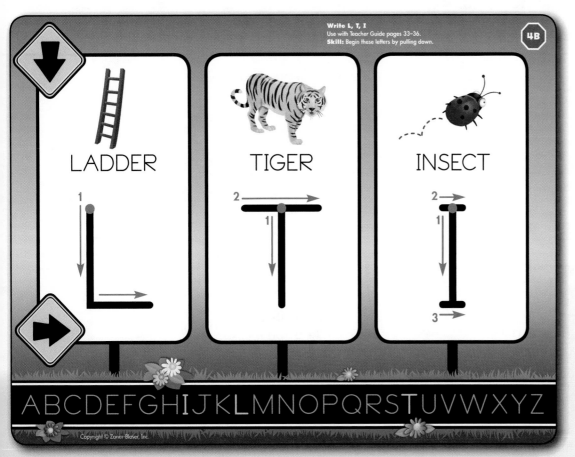

LADDER   TIGER   INSECT

ABCDEFGH**I**JK**L**MNOPQR**S**TUVWXYZ

Copyright © Zaner-Bloser, Inc.

Chant
Use this chant to remind children how to write in the sky.

Sky-Writing
I draw a paper in the sky.
I hold two fingers way up high.
I draw big lines and letters, too.
I'm sky-writing—so can you!

2 Center Time Days 3–5

*Choose multisensory activities for writing practice from the **Center Time** information on pages 18–19 or the activity below.*

Touch and Trace Supply Touch and Trace Letter Cards **L, T,** and **I,** blank paper, and crayons. Show how to trace with the pointer finger of the writing hand as the helper hand secures the card. Make sure to start at the arrow and to trace lines in the correct sequence. As they trace, children should say the name of each line aloud. They can then use paper and crayons to make rubbings and write the letters inside.

3 Play Time Days 3–5

*Use the **Play Time** information on page 20 and the idea below to introduce purposeful writing into children's dramatic play.*

Nature Explorer Explore the outdoors. If possible, supply for each child: a magnifying glass, a "notebook" made from small sheets of paper stapled together, and a crayon. Invite children to observe small things (bugs, blades of grass) and big things (clouds, trees) and to make drawings and notes.

Music, Mazes & More CD-ROM

Music for Movement
Sky-Writing (Track 1)
ABC Rap (Track 2)
Top to Bottom (Track 3)
I Pull Down (Track 9)

Optional Practice Pages
You may wish to use some of these practice pages in the writing center.

Mazes: Pages 1, 2, 5, 9
Picture/Letter Cards: Pages 13–16
Letters: Pages 39, 42, 50

35

Fun With Fundamentals

See pages 10–13 for more information about the development of these essential prewriting skills.

Developing Fine-Motor Skills

Allowing children to draw and write on a vertical surface, such as an easel or chalkboard, promotes shoulder strength and hand and wrist stability. Try drawing a picture on the chalkboard. Have children trace the lines of the picture with a paintbrush dipped in water.

Developing Letter Recognition

Display Alphabet Cards **L, T**, and **I**. Supply old newspapers and magazines, scissors, blank paper, glue, and crayons. Ask children to look through the newspapers and magazines and find two examples of each letter. After they cut out or tear the letters, children can glue them to blank paper and write the letters.

Developing Sound-Symbol Awareness

Divide children into two groups. Choose a child whose name contains **L** to lead one group and a child whose name contains **T** to lead the other group. Then read words, including **tiger, ladder, lemon, teddy bear, teeth, leaf, lap, tent, tickle,** and **laugh**. The leaders should help the groups decide if each word begins with their letter and, if so, applaud.

Developing Handwriting Skills

Handedness It is important to determine a dominant hand before children begin to write regularly. If a dominant hand is not trained, tasks will be divided between the two hands, and no one hand will gain more skill. To make the determination, observe the child in daily activities such as coloring, dressing, and eating. Provide materials at the middle of the body and see which hand reaches for them. Once hand dominance is determined, encourage the child to use that hand for writing. Place the writing tool near that hand.

Featured Letters

Objectives
- Recognize the letters **F, E, H**
- Write slide lines from left to right
- Write the letters **F, E, H**
- Listen to a story
- Develop oral language and writing skills

Kit Materials
- Group Time Card 5
- *Music, Mazes & More* CD-ROM
- Alphabet Cards **F, E, H**
- Magnetic Letters and Board
- Touch and Trace Letter Cards **F, E, H**
- Wikki Stix®

Classroom Materials
- Emery boards, paper, glue
- Pretend traffic signs
- Sidewalk chalk or masking tape
- Paper for tearing, crayons
- Scented lotion or other treats for children's hands
- Index cards, tape

Stroke Focus

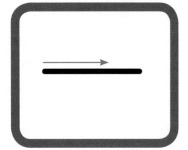

Slide.

Letter Focus

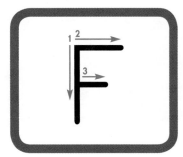

1. Pull down.
2. Slide.
3. Slide.

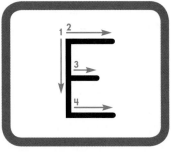

1. Pull down.
2. Slide.
3. Slide.
4. Slide.

1. Pull down.
2. Pull down.
3. Slide.

Teacher Tips

The horizontal stroke, or slide, is not difficult for many four- and five-year-olds. Point out slide lines in the environment (lines on the calendar, a table's edge, the monkey bars) and in children's drawings of people and buildings.

Preschoolers may write "embellished" **F**s and **E**s with as many as five or six slide lines! Don't be too concerned. Children will write the standard letterforms in time. Ask them to count the slides in **F** (2) and **E** (3).

Emphasize the left-to-right direction of slide lines. When children write a slide, place a green dot on the left to show the beginning point. Guide children's fingers in tracing slides from left to right. Tell them that we read across from left to right, too!

37

Stroke Story

Children act out motions shown in red.

Elephant wanted to slide down the sidewalk on roller-skates like his cousin. Grandma said it was his turn to try the skates.

"Will I fall down?" he asked Grandma.

"You might fall down while you are learning," she said. "Here, put these on to protect you."

She gave him a sturdy helmet, knee pads, and elbow and wrist pads. Elephant put them on, first the helmet (pretend to strap on helmet), then the knee pads (put on knee pads), then the elbow and wrist pads (put on elbow and wrist pads).

"Wait," said Elephant, and he ran inside. When he came out, he had two more hats on top of his helmet.

"You don't need those," Grandma laughed.

"Yes, I do," Elephant said. "With three hats, I'll be super safe!"

Elephant put a skate on his left foot (put on skate), then his right foot (put on skate). He stood up quickly, and fell down just as quickly (fall down).

"It's OK," said Grandma. "Try again." Elephant stood (stand up). He turned his body to the right and slid one foot forward, then the other. He didn't fall! He slid again carefully. He was doing it! (Slide several times from left to right.) Elephant kept trying until he could slide smoothly along.

38

Learn F, E, H
Use with Teacher Guide pages 37–40.
Skill: These letters have slide lines.

5A

F E H

ABCDEFGHIJKLMNOPQRSTUVWXYZ

Group Time Days 1–2

*Gather children together for group time. Use the **Group Time** information on pages 16–17 and the notes below.*

Group Time Card 5A
1. Warm up with a song. Choose one listed at right.
2. Tell the Stroke Story.
3. Trace the arrow under the elephant from left to right. Say "slide".
4. Sing "ABC Rap." Point to the target letters in yellow on the Alphabet Road.
5. Sky-write each slide line in **F**, **E**, and **H**. For each, say "slide".

Group Time Card 5B
1. Warm up with a song. Choose one listed at right.
2. Sing "ABC Rap." Point to the letters on the Alphabet Road. Clap when you come to **F**, **E**, and **H**.

3. Talk about the letter shapes. They look like parts of a ladder. **F** can be found inside **E**. Who has these letters in his or her name? Can these letters be found in the room? Read the word for each letter. Find the letter in the word.
4. Sky-write each letter several times, beginning at the green dot and following the arrows. Say the name of each line aloud.
5. Write an uppercase message to Elephant, such as HOLD ON TO YOUR HATS, ELEPHANT, using shared or interactive writing. Read the message together, pointing to letters, words, and spaces.

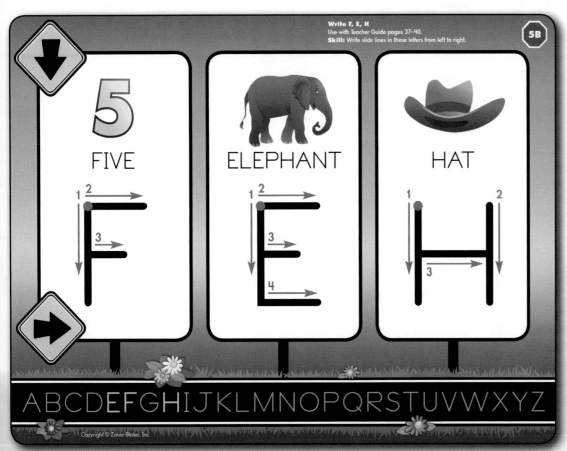

Write F, E, H
Use with Teacher Guide pages 37–40.
Skill: Write slide lines in these letters from left to right.

5B

FIVE

ELEPHANT

HAT

ABCD**EF**G**H**IJKLMNOPQRSTUVWXYZ

Copyright © Zaner-Bloser, Inc.

Chant

Use this chant to help children remember how to hold their crayon when they draw or write.

Hold Your Crayon

Crayon, crayon,
Do you want to write?
Jump in my fingers.
I won't hold you tight.

Lean on tall friend,
Pointer on top,
Rest on my thumb,
I won't let you drop.

Ring and pinky
Tuck in beside.
They touch the paper
As we take a ride.

② Center Time Days 3–5

*Choose multisensory activities for writing practice from the **Center Time** information on pages 18–19 or the activity below.*

Scratchy Letters Trace emery boards to make templates on sheets of paper for forming **F, E,** and **H.** Hint: Use two emery boards for vertical lines, so they are twice the length of horizontal lines. For example, use four boards to make **F**—two for the pull down line and two more for the slide lines. Children glue the boards on the templates to form letters. They use their fingers to trace each letter, saying "slide" for each slide line.

③ Play Time Days 3–5

*Use the **Play Time** information on page 20 and the idea below to introduce purposeful writing into children's dramatic play.*

Traffic If you have an area with a smooth floor, allow children to slide across it in their stocking feet. They can pretend to be driving cars or using roller skates as they slide. Provide materials for making traffic signs to regulate the travelers (LEFT, STOP). Some children might be police officers who write tickets for violators.

Music, Mazes & More
CD-ROM

Music for Movement

ABC Rap (Track 2)
Wake Up Fingers (Track 4)
Hold Your Crayon (Track 8)
Slide Along (Track 10)

Optional Practice Pages

You may wish to use some of these practice pages in the writing center.

Mazes: Pages 1, 2, 5, 9
Picture/Letter Cards: Pages 13, 15
Letters: Pages 35, 36, 38

39

Fun With Fundamentals

See pages 10–13 for more information about the development of these essential prewriting skills.

Developing Gross-Motor Skills

Use sidewalk chalk on the playground or strips of masking tape on the floor to form the letters **F, E,** and **H** at a large size. Place a green dot to show the starting position for each letter. Then invite children to swim like a Fish along the **F,** stomp like an Elephant along the **E,** and gallop like a Horse along the **H.**

Developing Fine-Motor Skills

Draw horizontal lines across paper for children to tear. Use a green dot to mark the left side of each line. Show how to secure the paper with the helper hand as the thumb and pointer finger of the dominant hand are used for tearing. Provide crayons so children can write their names on the torn paper strips.

Developing Spatial Awareness

Introduce children to their left hands. "Greet" each child's left hand. Throughout the day, give left hands special tasks to do and treats such as scented lotion, stickers, and interesting things to feel. Children can talk to their left hands, too. A few days later, give special attention to the right hand.

Developing Print Awareness

Act out reading and writing behaviors and have children tell you whether you are being a good reader/writer or not. For example, read the **ABC**s on the Group Time Card from right to left. *No, no, that's wrong,* the children will tell you. Write the slide lines in **E** from right to left. *No, that's not right either.* Write **F** and **H** correctly and get children's approval.

Developing Letter Recognition

Write **F, E,** or **H** on index cards. Tape one card to each child's back. Challenge children to ask each other questions that will help them guess their letter. They might ask, *How many slide lines does my letter have? How many pull down lines does my letter have? What sound does my letter make? What words have my letter?*

Featured Letters

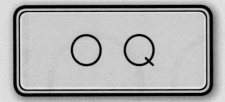

O Q

Objectives
- Recognize the letters **O, Q**
- Write circle back lines
- Write the letters **O, Q**
- Listen to a story
- Develop oral language and writing skills

Kit Materials
- Group Time Card 6
- *Music, Mazes & More* CD-ROM
- Alphabet Cards **O, Q**
- Magnetic Letters and Board
- Touch and Trace Letter Cards **O, Q**
- Wikki Stix®

Classroom Materials
- Clay, clay tools
- Supplies for a pretend aquarium exhibit
- Nylon rope, carpet tape
- String or yarn, **O**-shaped cereal
- Blank paper, crayons
- Bag

Stroke Focus

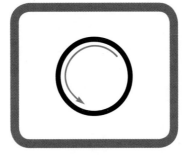

Circle back.

Letter Focus

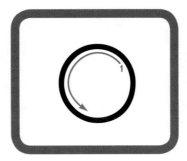

1. Circle back.

1. Circle back.
2. Slant right.

Teacher Tips

Many preschoolers use circles in their drawings. Explain that children should write their "best" circles for circle letters like **O** and **Q**.

Challenge them to write round circles that start and stop deliberately. Practice first by writing circles in the air, in a tray of sand or salt, or on the chalkboard with a wet sponge. Ask them to find the starting point for a circle back line (about 1:00) and say "start," then circle back continuously until they return to that point and say "stop."

When children write circles, they can imagine going around on a tire swing or stirring something in a bowl. This will encourage smooth circles.

Stroke Story

Children act out motions shown in red.

Octopus loved circles. She liked to hold her tentacles close together and swim around in sleek, fast circles. (Put fingers of writing hand together and move whole arm in a backward circle.) She liked to spread all her tentacles out and twirl in a circle. (Four children get together in a circle, with backs and shoulders together and eight arms stretched out; walk around in counterclockwise circle, waving arms.) She could even make a circle with each tentacle. (Stay in circle; children curve hands into circles.)

One day, Octopus found eight shiny circles on the bottom of the ocean—one for each tentacle! What could they be? Octopus looked closely. They were quarters! Maybe enough to buy a seaweed snack! Octopus was so happy she picked up the quarters and juggled them. In a circle, of course!

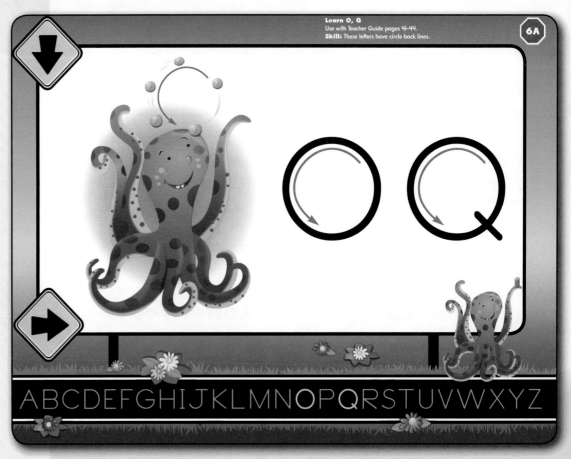

Learn O, Q
Use with Teacher Guide pages 41–44.
Skill: These letters have circle back lines.

6A

ABCDEFGHIJKLMN**O**P**Q**RSTUVWXYZ

Group Time Days 1–2

*Gather children together for group time. Use the **Group Time** information on pages 16–17 and the notes below.*

Group Time Card 6A
1. Warm up with a song. Choose one listed at right.
2. Tell the Stroke Story.
3. Trace the arrow beside the quarters in a counterclockwise motion. Say "circle back."
4. Sing "ABC Rap." Point to the target letters in yellow on the Alphabet Road.
5. Sky-write circle back lines in **O** and **Q**. For each, say "circle back."

Group Time Card 6B
1. Warm up with a song. Choose one listed at right.
2. Sing "ABC Rap." Point to the letters on the Alphabet Road. Clap when you come to **O** and **Q**.
3. Talk about the letter shapes. The letter **O** is a circle. **Q** is **O** with a "tail." Who has these letters in his or her name? Can these letters be found in the room? Read the word for each letter. Find the letter in the word.
4. Sky-write each letter several times, beginning at the green dot and following the arrows. Say the name of each line aloud.
5. Write an uppercase message, such as QUITE A GOOD TRICK, OCTOPUS, using shared or interactive writing. Read the message together, pointing to letters, words, and spaces.

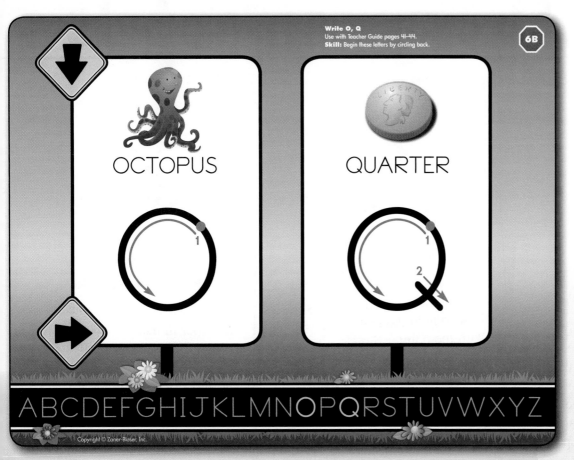

Write O, Q
Use with Teacher Guide pages 41–44.
Skill: Begin these letters by circling back.

6B

OCTOPUS

QUARTER

A B C D E F G H I J K L M N O P Q R S T U V W X Y Z

Chant
Use this chant to remind children how to write in the sky.

Sky-Writing
I draw a paper in the sky.
I hold two fingers way up high.
I draw big lines and letters, too.
I'm sky-writing—so can you!

 Center Time Days 3–5

*Choose multisensory activities for writing practice from the **Center Time** information on pages 18–19 or the activity below.*

Clay Circles Provide clay, Group Time Card 6 or Alphabet Cards **O** and **Q**, and plastic knives, toothpicks, or other marking tools. Show how to roll the clay into long ropes to be made into **O** and **Q** shapes on the cards. Use the tools to mark a starting point on the clay letters as well as lines, dots, or other textures. Ask children to use the pointer finger of the writing hand to trace the clay letter, saying "circle back." After lifting the clay **O** from the card, children may wish to shape a clay octopus to swim through the "hoop."

Play Time Days 3–5

*Use the **Play Time** information on page 20 and the idea below to introduce purposeful writing into children's dramatic play.*

Aquarium Let children make an aquarium in your classroom. Children may like to take on the roles of aquatic creatures, or they may decide to create them from paper, Wikki Stix, blocks, or toys. Help children think about how the exhibits will be organized and what information visitors will want to know. Provide text materials such as nonfiction books about aquatic life. Provide writing materials for making tickets, signs, and brochures.

Music, Mazes & More CD-ROM

Music for Movement
Sky-Writing (Track 1)
ABC Rap (Track 2)
Thumbs Up (Track 5)
Circle Song (Track 11)

Optional Practice Pages
You may wish to use some of these practice pages in the writing center.

Mazes: Pages 3, 7, 11
Picture/Letter Cards: Pages 14, 16
Letters: Pages 45, 47

Fun With Fundamentals

See pages 10–13 for more information about the development of these essential prewriting skills.

Developing Gross-Motor Skills

Lay a length of heavy, nylon rope on the floor in a large circle. Use carpet tape to secure the ends. Mark the starting position (at about 1:00) with a piece of tape. Invite children to balance as they walk along the rope in a counterclockwise motion.

Developing Fine-Motor Skills

Make necklaces from string or yarn and **O**-shaped cereal. Show how to hold the end of the string with the pointer finger and thumb of the writing hand. The helper hand holds the cereal. Poke the string through each cereal piece, grabbing it with the helper hand to thread it through. This motion helps develop the wrist and thumb.

Developing Print Awareness

Show how to fold 2–3 sheets of paper in half to make a book. Children can write a large **O** on each page, starting at the correct position and circling back. They can make each **O** into a picture—a wheel, a cookie, a face, etc. Encourage children to write labels for their pictures and to include a cover with the author's name.

Developing Letter Recognition

Put Letter Magnets in a bag, including **L, T, H, O, Q,** and other letters. On a magnetic surface, draw or tape an octopus body. Ask a child to draw a letter, name it, and name a line it contains (pull down, slide, circle, slant). Put up the magnet and let the child draw or tape a tentacle connecting it to the octopus. Repeat for all eight tentacles.

Developing Handwriting Skills

Sky-Writing Using the whole arm to sky-write helps children understand the motor pattern for each letter and begins the process of storing it in "muscle memory." It's good for gross-motor development and for kinesthetic learners. It's fun, too. Sing "Sky-Writing" (*Music, Mazes & More* CD-ROM, Track 1). Practice by sky-writing all kinds of lines and shapes. How about a squiggly line or a smiley face?

Featured Letters

Objectives
- Recognize the letters **C, G, S**
- Write circle back and curve back lines
- Write the letters **C, G, S**
- Listen to a story
- Develop oral language and writing skills

Kit Materials
- Group Time Card 7
- *Music, Mazes & More* CD-ROM
- Alphabet Cards **C, G, S**
- Magnetic Letters and Board
- Touch and Trace Letter Cards **C, G, S**
- Wikki Stix®

Classroom Materials
- Cardstock
- Party supplies
- Newspaper sheets
- Soap bubbles
- Old birthday cards
- Large gift bags

Stroke Focus

Circle back.

Curve back.

Letter Focus

I. Circle back.

I. Circle back.
Slide left.

I. Curve back.
Curve forward.

Teacher Tips

The letter **S** is troublesome for young children. Its shape is complex, formed from two opposite curves. To preschoolers' inexperienced eyes, its mirror image—a forward curve followed by a backward curve—may look close enough. In fact, reversed **S** may seem correct because its initial stroke follows the left-to-right rule. Letter reversals are common well into the elementary school years, and should not be a source of concern. With time and practice, children will master the spatial complexities of letters.

One way to avoid reversals is to help children get started in the correct direction. This is why **S** is grouped here with **C** and **G**, two other letters that begin with a counterclockwise motion. Children may note that **G** is another rule-breaker: Its slide stroke proceeds from right to left.

Stroke Story

Children act out motions shown in red.

Today is Goat's birthday. There is so much to do to get ready for the party, but everything is going wrong.

First, Goat couldn't find her special shoes. Dad said, "Circle back and look where you were." Goat walked in a slow circle. (Walk in a counterclockwise circle, looking all around.) She found them under the bed!

Next, Goat tried to blow up a balloon. When it was almost full, it slipped and circled around, making a loud noise until all the air was gone. (With the pointer finger of the writing hand, show the motion of a balloon circling back and deflating.) "Try again," said Dad, and Goat did. She blew up five balloons!

Next, Goat helped Dad with some ribbon. She tried to make a curl, but it looked all frazzled. "Like this," said Dad, and he helped her make a smooth curve. (With pointer finger, show curve back motion, like top of letter S.)

Next, Dad decorated the cake. The frosting was everywhere! Goat said, "Make a circle." "Good idea," said Dad. He circled the frosting around the edge of the cake. (With one fist on top of the other as if using a decorator bag, circle back.) It looked beautiful. It was going to be a great party!

Learn C, G, S
Use with Teacher Guide pages 45–48.
Skill: These letters have a circle back or curve back line.

7A

C G S

A B C D E F G H I J K L M N O P Q R S T U V W X Y Z

Group Time Days 1–2

*Gather children together for group time. Use the **Group Time** information on pages 16–17 and the notes below.*

Group Time Card 7A

1. Warm up with a song. Choose one listed at right.
2. Tell the Stroke Story.
3. Trace the arrow on the cake in a counterclockwise motion. Say "circle back" for a half-circle (as in **C**) or a three-quarters circle (as in **G**) and "curve back" for the beginning of a circle (as in **S**).
4. Sing "ABC Rap." Point to the target letters in yellow on the Alphabet Road.
5. Sky-write circle back and curve back lines in **C**, **G**, and **S**. For each, say "circle back" or "curve back."

Group Time Card 7B

1. Warm up with a song. Choose one listed at right.

2. Sing "ABC Rap." Point to the letters on the Alphabet Road. Clap when you come to **C**, **G**, and **S**.
3. Talk about the letter shapes. **C** is part of a circle, like a cookie with a bite taken out. The last part of **G**'s circle fell and became a slide line. **S** is a taken-apart circle that curves two ways—back and forward. Read the word for each letter. Find the letter in the word.
4. Sky-write each letter several times, beginning at the green dot and following the arrows. Say the name of each line aloud.
5. Write an uppercase message, such as CAN I HAVE SOME CAKE, GOAT?, using shared or interactive writing.

46

Write C, G, S
Use with Teacher Guide pages 45–48.
Skill: Begin these letters by circling back (C and G) or curving back (S).

7B

CAKE   GOAT   SUN

C   G   S

ABCDEFGHIJKLMNOPQRSTUVWXYZ

Chant

Use this chant to help children remember how to hold their crayon when they draw or write.

Hold Your Crayon

Crayon, crayon,
Do you want to write?
Jump in my fingers.
I won't hold you tight.

Lean on tall friend,
Pointer on top,
Rest on my thumb,
I won't let you drop.

Ring and pinky
Tuck in beside.
They touch the paper
As we take a ride.

2 Center Time Days 3–5

*Choose multisensory activities for writing practice from the **Center Time** information on pages 18–19 or the activity below.*

Birthday Words Cut sheets of cardstock in half to make 4 x 5 ½" cards. Write these words on the cards: CAKE, CANDLES, GAMES, GIFT, SING, SURPRISE. Put a green starting dot on each **C**, **G**, and **S**. If you wish, add picture cues and laminate the cards. Show how to read the words from left to right, finding **C**, **G**, and **S** and forming them on the cards with Wikki Stix®, while naming the lines aloud. Try making an audio recording of a story that includes the words. Children can find words and form letters as they listen to the story.

3 Play Time Days 3–5

*Use the **Play Time** information on page 20 and the idea below to introduce purposeful writing into children's dramatic play.*

Birthday Party Have a birthday party for a class pet, stuffed animal, or favorite book character. Suggest that children clean up the housekeeping area and decorate it for the party. Show how to staple paper cones for hats and decorate them. Provide materials for writing a guest list, birthday cards, gift tags, and a Happy Birthday banner.

Music, Mazes & More CD-ROM

Music for Movement
ABC Rap (Track 2)
Thumbkin (Track 6)
Hold Your Crayon (Track 8)
Circle Song (Track 11)

Optional Practice Pages
You may wish to use some of these practice pages in the writing center.

Mazes: Pages 3, 6, 7, 10–12
Picture/Letter Cards: Pages 13–16
Letters: Pages 33, 37, 49

47

Fun With Fundamentals

See pages 10–13 for more information about the development of these essential prewriting skills.

Developing Fine-Motor Skills

Build hand strength and control with these two fun activities. First, provide whole sheets of newspaper and challenge children to crush and scrunch them into balls using only the dominant hand. Play catch with the newspaper balls. Next, blow soap bubbles and challenge children to burst them by clapping their two hands together.

Developing Print Awareness

Make a class birthday book with 12 pages, one for each month. Children can write their name, age, and birthdate on the page that matches their birth month. Cover the book with a collage of old birthday cards. Put the book in the library center.

Developing Letter Recognition

Recognize children whose names contain **C**, **G**, or **S**. Provide name cards and ask them to highlight the target letters. Those with **C** in their names can stand and show their cards while the class sings: "Happy **C** day to you, happy **C** day to you…." Repeat for **G** and **S**.

Developing Sound-Symbol Awareness

Write **C**, **G**, and **S** on three large gift bags. Ask children to find small items in the classroom that begin with the **hard c, hard g**, or **/s/** sounds and place them in the matching bag. Items may include a cap, a gold crayon, and scissors. "Open" the gifts together and name each item, emphasizing its beginning sound.

Developing Handwriting Skills

Writing Grip Preschool is the ideal time to teach a comfortable and efficient writing grip. Monitor children's hands when writing and gently encourage good positioning, using the diagram on page 10 as a guide. Sing "Hold Your Crayon" (*Music, Mazes & More* CD-ROM, Track 8) to help children learn how to hold the crayon. Using small bits of crayon for writing will force children to "pinch" their fingers into a good position.

Featured Letters

P R

Objectives

- Recognize the letters **P, R**
- Write curve forward lines
- Write the letters **P, R**
- Listen to a story
- Develop oral language and writing skills

Kit Materials

- Group Time Card 8
- *Music, Mazes & More* CD-ROM
- Alphabet Cards **P, R**
- Magnetic Letters and Board
- Touch and Trace Letter Cards **P, R**
- Wikki Stix®

Classroom Materials

- Plastic or foam rectangular trays
- Shaving cream
- Red and blue food coloring
- Materials for a pretend painting business
- Scissors
- Construction paper

Stroke Focus

Curve forward.

Letter Focus

1. Pull down.
2. Curve forward.

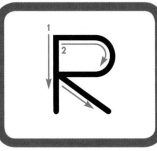

1. Pull down.
2. Curve forward.
3. Slant right.

Teacher Tips

Curves are modified circle parts. The curve forward shape introduced in this lesson can be demonstrated by pulling apart a circle made from a pipe cleaner or a Wikki Stix piece and gently compressing its shape. Children may enjoy writing the curve forward line by itself before combining it with pull down lines, as in **P** and **R**.

It is challenging for young children to begin and end the curve precisely on the "stem," or pull down line, in these letters. Don't be concerned if children's curves extend beyond the boundaries of the vertical lines. With time, children will start and stop the writing tool more deliberately.

Stroke Story

Children act out motions shown in red.

Pig loved to paint, especially with red paint. He painted pictures of red houses and red fences, red telephone poles and red bookshelves. (Paint some of these things in the air, with the writing hand holding a pretend paintbrush.)

Pig's friend asked, "Why do all your paintings have straight lines?" Pig had never noticed this before. He did like to pull his brush down to make tall, straight lines. (Paint a pull down line.) And he liked to slide his brush across to make long, straight lines, too. (Paint a slide line.) "That is just how I paint," said Pig. And he went on painting pictures of red steps, red windows, and red chairs.

One day a bird swooped by. "I would like to paint that swooping shape," said Pig. When he did, his brush made a curved line. (Paint a curve forward, to the right.) Pig made more and more curves. He painted the curved shape of a leaf blowing. (Curve forward.) He painted the curved shape of his toy race car making a turn. (Curve forward.) Pig liked the new, curved lines. "Hmm," said Pig. "Maybe tomorrow I will paint something purple."

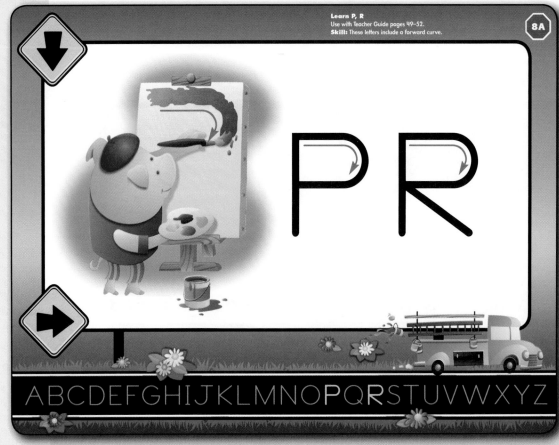

Learn P, R
Use with Teacher Guide pages 49–52.
Skill: These letters include a forward curve.

8A

ABCDEFGHIJKLMNOPQRSTUVWXYZ

Group Time Days 1–2

*Gather children together for group time. Use the **Group Time** information on pages 16–17 and the notes below.*

Group Time Card 8A
1. Warm up with a song. Choose one listed at right.
2. Tell the Stroke Story.
3. Trace the arrow beside the brush stroke. Say "curve forward."
4. Sing "ABC Rap." Point to the target letters in yellow on the Alphabet Road.
5. Sky-write curve forward lines in **P** and **R**. For each, say "curve forward."

Group Time Card 8B
1. Warm up with a song. Choose one listed at right.
2. Sing "ABC Rap." Point to the letters on the Alphabet Road. Clap when you come to **P** and **R**.
3. Talk about the letter shapes. **P** can be seen inside **R**. Curves are parts of circles that have been squished. Who has these letters in his or her name? Read the word for each letter. Find the letter in the word.
4. Sky-write each letter several times, beginning at the green dot and following the arrows. Say the name of each line aloud.
5. Write an uppercase message, such as REALLY GOOD PICTURE, PIG, using shared or interactive writing. Read the message together, pointing to letters, words, and spaces.

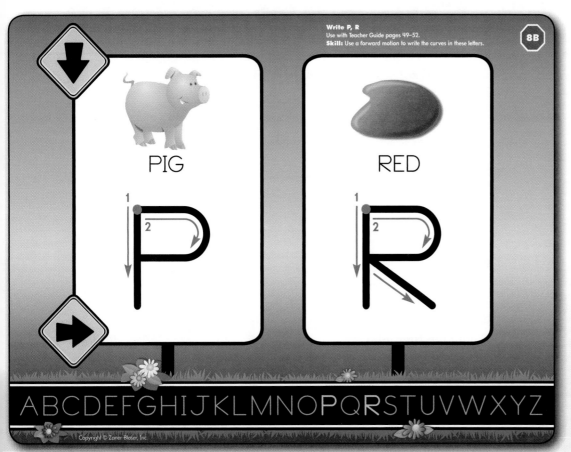

Write P, R
Use with Teacher Guide pages 49–52.
Skill: Use a forward motion to write the curves in these letters.

8B

PIG

RED

ABCDEFGHIJKLMNOPQRSTUVWXYZ

Chant

Use this chant to help children remember to use the helper hand when they draw or write.

Helper Hand

Helper hand, helper hand,
Help me write.
Stay flat and hold my paper
As we move from left to right.

Center Time Days 3–5

*Choose multisensory activities for writing practice from the **Center Time** information on pages 18–19 or the activity below.*

Finger Paint Provide plastic or foam rectangular trays. In each tray, dispense shaving cream and either red food coloring or red and blue food coloring to make purple. Children should use the pointer finger of the writing hand to mix the color and smooth out the cream to make a surface for finger painting. Show how to use the shape of the tray to help write **P** and **R** in the cream with the pointer finger. Both letters begin at the upper left corner of the tray. Their curve forward strokes fill the space all the way to the right edge. **R**'s slant stroke goes down to the lower right corner.

Play Time Days 3–5

*Use the **Play Time** information on page 20 and the idea below to introduce purposeful writing into children's dramatic play.*

Painters, Inc. Help children set up a painting business outside. Provide paintbrushes of all sizes and plastic cups or tubs. Fill the containers with water so the painters can spruce up the playground equipment or outdoor area. Also, establish an office with a play phone so that customers can call with painting jobs. Writing materials will be needed for taking phone messages, assigning jobs, and sending and paying bills. Color names may be written on the cups of paint.

Music, Mazes & More
CD-ROM

Music for Movement

ABC Rap (Track 2)
Top to Bottom (Track 3)
My Two Hands (Track 7)
Circle Song (Track 11)

Optional Practice Pages

You may wish to use some of these practice pages in the writing center.

Mazes: Pages 6, 10, 12
Picture/Letter Cards: Pages 14, 16
Letters: Pages 46, 48

Fun With Fundamentals

See pages 10–13 for more information about the development of these essential prewriting skills.

Developing Fine-Motor Skills

Learning how to use scissors enhances children's ability to hold and control a writing tool. The middle finger and thumb are placed in the scissor handles no farther than the first joint. The pointer finger is held against the scissor shaft to aid in closing the blades while supporting the scissors. Help children remember how the scissors fit on the hand by marking lines across the inside joints of the middle finger and thumb. Before cutting, play puppet games. Hold a pair of scissors yourself and open and close them in a pattern, such as slow/fast or wide/slight. Ask children to make their scissors repeat what yours "said."

Developing Letter Recognition

Give a cheer for children whose names contain **P** or **R**. Spread Alphabet Cards on the floor and shout (for Peter): "Give me a **P**." Children find the **P** card and shout **P**. Repeat for each letter, then shout "What's that spell?" Children respond, *Peter*!

Developing Gross-Motor Skills

Play music while children move like animals that begin with **P** and **R**: pigs, rabbits, ponies, reindeer, parrots, and rats.

Developing Sound-Symbol Awareness

Use construction paper to make two paintbrushes for each child—one with red paint (labeled **R**), and one with purple paint (labeled **P**). Pronounce words such as **red, purple, paint, pig, rain**, and **roof**. Emphasize the beginning sound. Ask children to hold up the paintbrush that matches each word's beginning sound.

Developing Handwriting Skills

Helper Hand As hand dominance becomes well-developed, make children aware of the importance of the non-writing hand, or helper hand. Its job is to be on the tabletop, holding and shifting the paper. Develop skills through activities that use the hands in different ways. Examples: holding a bowl while stirring, holding a box while reaching in, holding a cup while pouring.

Featured Letters

Objectives
- Recognize the letters **D, B**
- Write curve forward lines
- Write the letters **D, B**
- Listen to a story
- Develop oral language and writing skills

Kit Materials
- Group Time Card 9
- *Music, Mazes & More* CD-ROM
- Alphabet Cards **D, B**
- Magnetic Letters and Board
- Story Journals
- Touch and Trace Letter Cards **D, B**
- Wikki Stix®

Classroom Materials
- Soft pointer
- Camera
- Pretend dentist office supplies
- Tub with scissors and heavyweight materials for cutting
- Tic-tac-toe boards, green crayons
- Drawing paper and crayons
- Self-adhesive labels

Stroke Focus

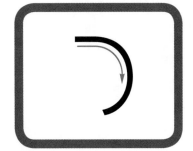

Curve forward.

Letter Focus

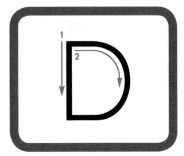

1. Pull down.
2. Curve forward.

1. Pull down.
2. Curve forward.
   Curve forward.

Teacher Tips

Children's experiences with writing **D** and **B** will be similar to their experiences with **P** and **R**. Joining curve strokes to the central pull down line at the left of each letter may present challenges, especially for **B**, which has two curves. Don't be concerned if the two curves don't touch when children write **B**. This will come with time and practice.

To discourage children from writing small, cramped curves, have them write curves and curve letters at a large size by sky-writing or writing on a chalkboard or marker board. Admire the smooth, round curves in their writing.

Stroke Story

Children act out motions shown in red.

Every night, Bear's mom brushes Bear's teeth. Mom says, "Open wide," and then she uses Bear's toothbrush to make each tooth shine. This makes Bear angry. She wants to brush her teeth all by herself. "You're not old enough," Mom argues. "Yes I am," Bear says. "I know how to do it. Watch me."

Mom sits on the tub to watch. Bear squeezes some toothpaste on the brush. (Squeeze on toothpaste.) She brushes her big, bear teeth as she curves her brush around. (Act out brushing with a forward curving motion to the right.) Bear rinses her mouth and puts the tooth brushing things away. She picks up her hairbrush and combs the fur on top of her head into a smooth curl. (Brush hair with a forward curve.) "Good job!" Mom says.

The next day, Bear has a dentist appointment. Mom is in a hurry to go. She starts to drive down the street. (With pointer finger, show car's path of driving to the right.) "Wait!" says Bear. "I forgot to brush my teeth." Mom turns the car around to go back home. (Show path of car making a U turn and going back.) "Good remembering," says Mom. "You are old enough to do it yourself."

Learn D, B
Use with Teacher Guide pages 53–56.
Skill: These letters include forward curves.

9A

DENTIST

ABCDEFGHIJKLMNOPQRSTUVWXYZ

Group Time Days 1–2

*Gather children together for group time. Use the **Group Time** information on pages 16–17 and the notes below.*

Group Time Card 9A

1. Warm up with a song. Choose one listed at right.
2. Tell the Stroke Story.
3. Trace the arrow beside the bear's hand in a curve to the right. Say "curve forward."
4. Sing "ABC Rap." Point to the target letters in yellow on the Alphabet Road.
5. Sky-write curve forward lines in **D** and **B**. For each, say "curve forward."

Group Time Card 9B

1. Warm up with a song. Choose one listed at right.
2. Sing "ABC Rap." Point to the letters on the Alphabet Road. Clap when you come to **D** and **B**.
3. Talk about the letter shapes. **D** has one fat curve that begins and ends on the pull down line. **B**'s curves look like squashed balloons touching in the middle. Who has these letters in his or her name? Can these letters be found in the room? Read the word for each letter. Find the letter in the word.
4. Sky-write each letter several times, beginning at the green dot and following the arrows. Say the name of each line aloud.
5. Write an uppercase message, such as GOOD JOB, BEAR, using shared or interactive writing. Read the message together, pointing to letters, words, and spaces.

Write D, B
Use with Teacher Guide pages 53–56.
Skill: Use a forward motion to write the curves in these letters.

9B

DOOR

BEAR

D

B

A B C D E F G H I J K L M N O P Q R S T U V W X Y Z

Copyright © Zaner-Bloser, Inc.

Chant
Use this chant with uppercase or lowercase alphabet cards to help children with letter recognition.

I Spy a Letter
I spy a letter.
Can you see?
It might be A.
It could be Z.
Here's a clue:
It looks like _____.
Here's a clue:
It sounds like _____.
Can you guess it?
It's a letter you've met.
It's part of
The alphabet!

2. Center Time Days 3–5

*Choose multisensory activities for writing practice from the **Center Time** information on pages 18–19 or the activity below.*

Body Letters Ask groups of children to form **D** or **B** with their bodies on the floor, using Alphabet Cards as a guide. When each group has formed its letter, let a volunteer trace it in the correct direction using a soft pointer, such as a feather taped to a yardstick. Tell children to try not to laugh, and ruin the letter's shape, while they are being traced! The tracing volunteer should name each line in the letter. From above, take "aerial" photographs of the completed letters. Try this with other letters children know, too.

3. Play Time Days 3–5

*Use the **Play Time** information on page 20 and the idea below to introduce purposeful writing into children's dramatic play.*

Dentist Play dentist's office. Offer roles of dentists, assistants, hygienists, receptionists, and patients. An examination chair may be set up with a tray of block tools beside it. The waiting room should be equipped with books about going to the dentist and posters about the importance of tooth brushing. Provide writing materials for making appointment reminders, calendars, posters, and patient charts.

Music, Mazes & More CD-ROM

Music for Movement
ABC Rap (Track 2)
Top to Bottom (Track 3)
Thumbs Up (Track 5)
Circle Song (Track 11)

Optional Practice Pages
You may wish to use some of these practice pages in the writing center.

Mazes: Pages 1, 2, 5, 6, 9–12
Picture/Letter Cards:
    Pages 13, 15
Letters: Pages 32, 34

55

Fun With Fundamentals

See pages 10–13 for more information about the development of these essential prewriting skills.

Developing Fine-Motor Skills

Continue to develop children's scissor skills. Stock a shallow storage tub with cutting supplies and make it available throughout the day. Include scissors and heavyweight cutting materials such as drinking straws (to snip into bits), old playing cards, magazine inserts, and manila folders. Don't provide regular paper yet—it requires more assistance from the helper hand. Encourage children to cut short, one-cut straight lines before proceeding to longer multiple-cut straight lines, wavy lines, shapes, and circles.

Developing Spatial Awareness

For each pair of children, provide a square tic-tac-toe board on paper. Have them color over the first three vertical lines in the grid with green crayon so that the left side of each of the nine smaller boxes is green. Remind children that **D** and **B** begin with a pull down line at the left/green side of each box. Children can use the board to play tic-tac-toe with **D**s and **B**s in place of **X**s and **O**s.

Developing Print Awareness

Have each child tell you a short story about his or her experiences going to the dentist. Write the story in one or two sentences at the bottom of a large sheet of drawing paper. Examine the sentences with children, pointing out letters, words, and spaces. Let children illustrate the stories with crayons and "read" them to the class.

Developing Letter Recognition

Write familiar letters on self-adhesive labels and let each child wear one. Throughout the day, choose children for special tasks—such as leading a line, answering a question, or going to a center—by calling out their letters.

Developing Sound-Symbol Awareness

Put **D** and **B** Letter Magnets on a magnetic surface that children pass frequently during the day—a door jamb, water fountain, or filing cabinet. Every time children pass this location, they must touch each letter and say a word that begins with its sound.

Featured Letters

K N M

Objectives
- Recognize the letters **K, N, M**
- Write slant right lines
- Write the letters **K, N, M**
- Listen to a story
- Develop oral language and writing skills

Kit Materials
- Group Time Card 10
- *Music, Mazes & More* CD-ROM
- Alphabet Cards **K, N, M**
- Magnetic Letters and Board
- Touch and Trace Letter Cards **K, N, M**
- Wikki Stix®

Classroom Materials
- Large craft sticks, construction paper, glue, crayons
- Collage materials: Kix® cereal, dry noodles, mini marshmallows
- Materials for a pretend gym
- Flashlight
- Hula hoop, beanbags
- Rulers or dowels
- Index cards
- Paper circles, curling ribbon

Stroke Focus

Slant right.

Letter Focus

1. Pull down.
2. Slant left.
   Slant right.

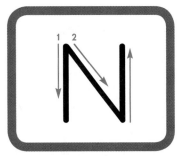

1. Pull down.
2. Slant right.
   Push up straight.

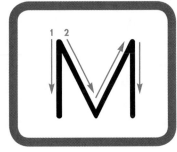

1. Pull down.
2. Slant right.
   Slant up.
   Pull down.

Teacher Tips

This is the first of several lessons that introduce slanted lines. Although the featured letters, **K, N,** and **M,** contain several kinds of slant lines, the slant right line is emphasized. This is the simplest slant line to write because it follows the top-to-bottom and left-to-right rules.

When writing slant lines, children are often unsure of where to start and where to aim. Provide plenty of support as children write slant lines by using green and red dots to indicate starting and stopping points. Help children understand through play and body movements that slant lines are leaning lines. Don't become concerned if children's slant lines are too long, or if they don't join smoothly in letters. Praise their efforts to write lines that slant in specific directions.

Stroke Story

Children act out motions shown in red.

Kangaroo was going to his first karate class. His friends Flamingo, Elephant, and Giraffe already went to classes at the *dojo*, or karate school, and now he would join them. He was excited to be wearing his uniform, or *gi*.

The teacher asked the students to kick one leg out powerfully to the right. Kangaroo tried to kick, but instead, he jumped. (Jump.) Kangaroo was used to jumping. It was hard to do something new. He tried again to kick, but only jumped. (Jump.)

Kangaroo's friends could tell he was frustrated. "Like this," said Flamingo, and she kicked out her long leg so her three-toed foot slanted to the floor. (Turn to the right and kick out dominant foot.) "Like this," said Elephant, and she kicked her short, strong leg. (Kick to right.) "Like this," said Giraffe, and he bent his knee and kicked his hoof to the right. (Kick to right.)

"I'll try again," said Kangaroo. This time he did it. His leg kicked out powerfully. (Kick to right.) "Good!" said his friends. "Try it again." Kangaroo kicked again and shouted *kiai* (pronounced key-eye) to show his spirit. (Kick to the right and shout kiai.)

Learn K, N, M
Use with Teacher Guide pages 57–60.
Skill: Each of these letters has a slant right stroke.

10A

ABCDEFGHIJ**K**L**MN**OPQRSTUVWXYZ

Group Time Days 1–2

*Gather children together for group time. Use the **Group Time** information on pages 16–17 and the notes below.*

Group Time Card 10A
1. Warm up with a song. Choose one listed at right.
2. Tell the Stroke Story.
3. Trace the arrow beside the kangaroo's leg. Say "slant right."
4. Sing "ABC Rap." Point to the target letters in yellow on the Alphabet Road.
5. Sky-write slant right lines in **K, N,** and **M.** For each, say "slant right."

Group Time Card 10B
1. Warm up with a song. Choose one listed at right.
2. Sing "ABC Rap." Point to the letters on the Alphabet Road. Clap when you come to **K, N,** and **M.**

3. Talk about the letter shapes. **K** looks like a person with an arm and leg kicked out. **M** looks like a cat's ears. All the letters have pull down lines and slant lines. Who has these letters in his or her name? Read the word for each letter. Find the letter in the word.
4. Sky-write each letter several times, beginning at the green dot and following the arrows. Say the name of each line aloud.
5. Write an uppercase message, such as DON'T JUMP, KANGAROO, KICK, using shared or interactive writing. Read the message together, pointing to letters, words, and spaces.

Write K, N, M
Use with Teacher Guide pages 56–60.
Skill: Slant down to the right in each letter.

10B

KANGAROO

9 NINE

MEDAL

ABCDEFGHIJ**KLMN**OPQRSTUVWXYZ

Copyright © Zaner-Bloser, Inc.

Chant

Use this chant to help children remember to use the helper hand when they draw or write.

Helper Hand

Helper hand, helper hand,
Help me write.
Stay flat and hold my paper
As we move from left to right.

2 Center Time Days 3–5

*Choose multisensory activities for writing practice from the **Center Time** information on pages 18–19 or the activity below.*

Craft Stick Letters Provide large craft sticks, glue, and construction paper. Children can glue craft sticks to form the shape of each letter (**K, N, M**) on a sheet of construction paper. Help them use green crayons to add a starting dot for each letter and an arrow on each slant right line. Children can trace the letters as they name each line. Finally, provide Kix® cereal, dry noodles, and mini marshmallows. Let children glue the items to the letter with the matching sound to make a collage.

3 Play Time Days 3–5

*Use the **Play Time** information on page 20 and the idea below to introduce purposeful writing into children's dramatic play.*

Kid Gym Establish a pretend gym that offers classes in karate, gymnastics, and exercising. Children may lead classes or participate in them. Play music that will inspire children to move and offer books or posters about physical activities. Provide writing materials for making class sign-up sheets, schedules, play money, and awards.

Music, Mazes & More CD-ROM

Music for Movement
ABC Rap (Track 2)
Top to Bottom (Track 3)
Thumbkin (Track 6)
Slant Dance (Track 12)

Optional Practice Pages
You may wish to use some of these practice pages in the writing center.

Mazes: Pages 1, 2, 4, 5, 8, 9
Picture/Letter Cards: Pages 13–16
Letters: Pages 41, 43, 44

59

Fun With Fundamentals

See pages 10–13 for more information about the development of these essential prewriting skills.

Developing Fine-Motor Skills

For development of eye muscles, have children lie on the floor while you shine a flashlight on the ceiling. Children's eyes will follow the light as you trace vertical, horizontal, and diagonal lines.

For development of hand-eye coordination, place a hula hoop flat on the floor and have children try to throw bean bags inside, gradually increasing distance.

Developing Spatial Awareness

Provide for each child a ruler, dowel, Tinker Toy® stick, or other straight object. Discuss concepts of up/down and left/right. Then give directions such as "Slant your stick down to the left" or "Slant up to the right." Add an auditory component by devising a sound effect for each motion/direction.

Developing Letter Recognition

Write **K, N, M** and other familiar letters on pairs of index cards and distribute to children. On a signal, children scramble to find their letter partners. Mix up the cards and play again.

Developing Sound-Symbol Awareness

Make a medal for each child by stapling a paper circle to a length of curling ribbon. Write **K, M, N** and other familiar letters on the circles. Then name a letter, pronounce its sound, and ask a volunteer to think of a word that begins with the sound. Place the medal around the child's neck as a reward for a correct response.

Developing Handwriting Skills

Children are typically able to write lines and shapes in this developmental sequence: dots, straight lines and squares, circles and curves, and diagonal lines and triangles. As children work with slant lines, keep in mind that diagonals are difficult for young children. Provide support by placing a green dot where the slant line should begin and a red dot where it should end. Help children see slant lines in the environment.

Featured Letters

Objectives
- Recognize the letters **V, W**
- Write slant up lines
- Write the letters **V, W**
- Listen to a story
- Develop oral language and writing skills

Kit Materials
- Group Time Card 11
- *Music, Mazes & More* CD-ROM
- Alphabet Cards **V, W**
- Magnetic Letters and Board
- Touch and Trace Letter Cards **V, W**
- Wikki Stix®
- Group Time Card 25A

Classroom Materials
- Materials for a pretend amusement park
- Piano or xylophone
- Scarves
- Sticky notes
- Letter Bingo cards
- Vanilla wafer cookies

Stroke Focus

Slant up.

Letter Focus

I. Slant right.
Slant up.

I. Slant right.
Slant up.
Slant right.
Slant up.

Teacher Tips

This lesson focuses on slant up lines, which are written from bottom left to top right. Slant up lines follow slant right lines in the featured letters, **V** and **W**. These letters are written with a down-and-up motion. Help children become comfortable with this movement by writing the down-up pattern continuously across the chalkboard, in a tray of sand or salt, or as a decorative border for pictures they draw. To discourage tight, cramped letters, emphasize that there should be plenty of room inside the "cone" of **V** for a scoop of vanilla ice cream and room inside **W** for a wave of water.

WWWWWWWW

Stroke Story

Children act out motions shown in red.

When Walrus was four years old, she and Grandpa rode a roller coaster with one big hill. It was called Thundering Volcano. Walrus loved it. She rode it two times. The car zoomed down the big hill, then back up to the top. (Extend pointer and middle fingers of helper hand to make a V. Use the pointer finger of the writing hand to trace the path of the roller coaster: down the inside of the middle finger and back up the inside of the pointer finger. Repeat.) At the gift shop, she got a vest that said "I Rode Thundering Volcano."

When Walrus was five years old, she and Grandpa rode a roller coaster with two big hills. It was called Wild Waterfall. Walrus loved it, too. She rode it three times. The car zoomed down the first big hill, then up to the top. Then, even faster, it zoomed down the second big hill and back to the top. (Extend pointer, middle, and ring fingers of helper hand to make a W. Use the pointer finger of the writing hand to trace the path of the roller coaster: down the inside of the ring finger, up and down the middle finger, and back up the inside of the pointer finger. Repeat twice.) This time, Walrus got a whistle that said "I Rode Wild Waterfall."

I wonder what Walrus will ride when she is six?

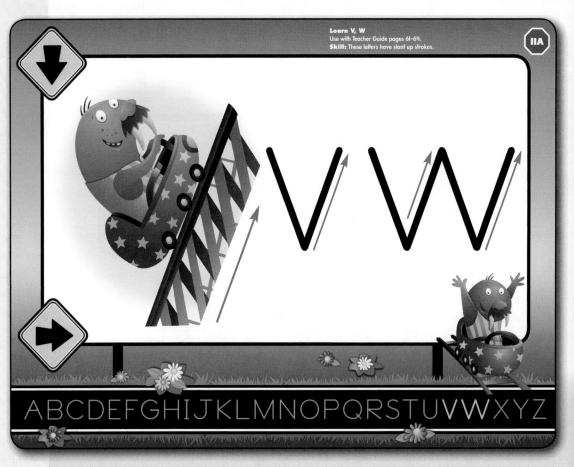

Learn V, W
Use with Teacher Guide pages 61–64.
Skill: These letters have slant up strokes.

IIA

ABCDEFGHIJKLMNOPQRSTUVWXYZ

Group Time Days 1–2

*Gather children together for group time. Use the **Group Time** information on pages 16–17 and the notes below.*

Group Time Card IIA

1. Warm up with a song. Choose one listed at right.
2. Tell the Stroke Story.
3. Trace the arrow beside the roller coaster from bottom to top. Say "slant up."
4. Sing "ABC Rap." Point to the target letters in yellow on the Alphabet Road.
5. Sky-write slant up lines in **V** and **W**. For each, say "slant up."

Group Time Card IIB

1. Warm up with a song. Choose one listed at right.
2. Sing "ABC Rap." Point to the letters on the Alphabet Road. Clap when you come to **V** and **W**.
3. Talk about the letter shapes. **V** looks like a valley between two mountainsides. **W** is two **V**s put together. Can you see **V** inside **W**? Read the word for each letter. Find the letter in the word. Who has these letters in his or her name?
4. Sky-write each letter several times, beginning at the green dot and following the arrows. Say the name of each line aloud.
5. Write an uppercase message, such as WALRUS LOVES VERY WILD RIDES, using shared or interactive writing. Point to letters, words, and spaces.

Write V, W
Use with Teacher Guide pages 61–64.
Skill: For slant up strokes, push from the bottom up to the right.

IIB

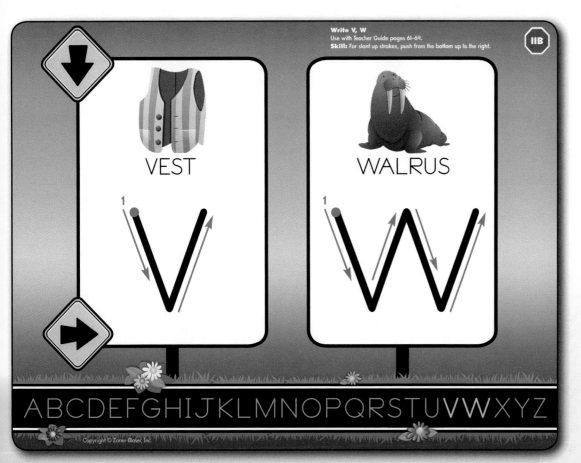

VEST

WALRUS

ABCDEFGHIJKLMNOPQRSTUVWXYZ

Chant

Use this chant with uppercase or lowercase alphabet cards to help children with letter recognition.

I Spy a Letter

I spy a letter.
Can you see?
It might be A.
It could be Z.
Here's a clue:
It looks like _____.
Here's a clue:
It sounds like _____.
Can you guess it?
It's a letter you've met.
It's part of
The alphabet!

Center Time Days 3–5

*Choose multisensory activities for writing practice from the **Center Time** information on pages 18–19 or the activity below.*

Window Words Let children decorate a window with Wikki Stix. They can use one Wikki Stix piece per line to make patterns of continuous slant right/slant up lines. Above the pattern, let children use Wikki Stix to write the word **WAVE**. Have them choose a contrasting color to show the **W** and **V** in **WAVE**. Encourage children to trace the Wikki Stix with the pointer finger of the writing hand in a slant right, slant up pattern.

Play Time Days 3–5

*Use the **Play Time** information on page 20 and the idea below to introduce purposeful writing into children's dramatic play.*

Amusement Park Let children create an amusement park with attractions such as Ride the Swings, Throw Balls in the Basket, and Jump on Mats. Children may want to write exciting names for the attractions on signs they make. Also provide materials for making tickets and writing safety rules for each ride.

Music, Mazes & More CD-ROM

Music for Movement
ABC Rap (Track 2)
Wake Up Fingers (Track 4)
Hold Your Crayon (Track 8)
Slant Dance (Track 12)

Optional Practice Pages
You may wish to use some of these practice pages in the writing center.

Mazes: Pages 4, 8
Picture/Letter Cards: Pages 14, 16
Letters: Pages 52, 53

Fun With Fundamentals

See pages 10–13 for more information about the development of these essential prewriting skills.

Developing Fine-Motor Skills

Writing is one of many skills that require children to reach across the midline of the body. To help children become comfortable with this habit, try these ideas. 1) Place children in front of a piano or xylophone and ask them to strike the farthest left keys with the right hand and the farthest right keys with the left hand. Monitor to make sure children don't switch hands at midline. 2) When painting at an easel, encourage children to paint long horizontal lines from edge to edge and long diagonal lines from corner to corner without switching hands.

Developing Spatial Awareness

Play lively music as children dance with scarves held in the writing hand. As they dance, ask them to move their scarves up to the right, down to the left, around in a circle, etc.

Developing Letter Recognition

Display Group Time Card 25A. Give clues about familiar letters based on their lines and shapes. For example, say "This letter looks like two **V**s together" (**W**), "This letter has two curves that touch in the middle," (**B**) or "This letter has a big circle line and a little slant line" (**Q**). For each correct response, allow the child to cover the letter with a sticky note.

Developing Sound-Symbol Awareness

Play Letter Bingo. Prepare cards with large 3 × 3 grids and write **V, W,** or another familiar letter in each square. As you call out letters, let players mark their cards with vanilla wafer cookies. For each letter children mark, have them call out a word they know that begins with its sound. Play until all children have shouted *Bingo.*

Developing Handwriting Skills

Learning Styles Writing is an essential skill for all children. Some children learn best through auditory instruction (naming lines in letters). Some learn best through visual instruction (looking at letter models and arrows). Others learn best through tactile/kinesthetic instruction (using Touch and Trace Letter Cards and sky-writing). Engage all children by using a variety of methods for teaching writing.

Featured Letters

A X

Objectives

- Recognize the letters **A, X**
- Write slant left lines
- Write the letters **A, X**
- Listen to a story
- Develop oral language and writing skills

Kit Materials

- Group Time Card 12
- *Music, Mazes & More* CD-ROM
- Alphabet Cards **A, X**
- Magnetic Letters and Board
- Touch and Trace Letter Cards **A, X**
- Wikki Stix®

Classroom Materials

- Flat, textured materials such as sandpaper, burlap, felt, plastic cross-stitch canvas
- Chart paper
- Supplies for the Alphabet Restaurant
- Blank paper and crayons
- Playground cones
- Sentence strips

Stroke Focus

Slant left.

Letter Focus

1. Slant left.
2. Slant right.
3. Slide.

1. Slant right.
2. Slant left.

Teacher Tips

The slant left line may be familiar to children as the first stroke in uppercase **A**. However, children may be tempted to start **A** at the bottom, slanting up and then down to form its tent-like shape. Remind children that letters start at the top. The correct sequence for **A** is: Slant down to the left. Lift. Slant down to the right. Lift. Slide across. Instilling this habit will avoid cramped and tilting **A**s.

To practice slant lines, suggest that children include triangles in their drawings. Triangles, too, should begin at the top.

Stroke Story

Children act out motions shown in red.

Alligator and Ox went to play at their cousin's house in the country. They played outside all day. Their favorite thing was playing with the wheelbarrow. Alligator had never seen one before. His cousin told him it was a tool for moving dirt and other heavy things. It had one wheel in front. If you held the handles and tipped it up on its wheel, it was easy to push. When an adult was watching, the kids were allowed to ride in the wheelbarrow and push each other around.

When Alligator and Ox got home, they missed their cousin and the wheelbarrow game. Alligator said, "Let's play wheelbarrow by ourselves." Alligator held Ox's feet like two handles. Ox put her hands on the floor to be the wheel. Ox's body slanted down. Alligator steered the wheelbarrow while Ox walked on her hands. It was fun! Next it was Alligator's turn to slant and walk on his hands. Can YOU do it, too? (Try wheelbarrow walking in groups of three; two children play while the third traces the slant left line, from feet to head, created as the wheelbarrow walker goes to the left. Change roles so all have a chance to be the wheelbarrow.)

Learn A, X
Use with Teacher Guide pages 65–68.
Skill: These letters have a slant left stroke.

12A

A X

ABCDEFGHIJKLMNOPQRSTUVWXYZ

Group Time Days 1–2

*Gather children together for group time. Use the **Group Time** information on pages 16–17 and the notes below.*

Group Time Card 12A

1. Warm up with a song. Choose one listed at right.
2. Tell the Stroke Story.
3. Trace the arrow beside the wheelbarrow. Say "slant left."
4. Sing "ABC Rap." Point to the target letters in yellow on the Alphabet Road.
5. Sky-write slant left lines in **A** and **X**. For each, say "slant left."

Group Time Card 12B

1. Warm up with a song. Choose one listed at right.
2. Sing "ABC Rap." Point to the letters on the Alphabet Road. Clap when you come to **A** and **X**.

3. Talk about the letter shapes. **A** looks like the end of a swing set or like a tent. **X** is two slant lines, criss-crossed. Who has these letters in his or her name? Can these letters be found in the room? Read the word for each letter. Find the letter in the word.
4. Sky-write each letter several times, beginning at the green dot and following the arrows. Say the name of each line aloud.
5. Write an uppercase message, such as WE PLAYED LIKE ALLIGATOR AND OX, using shared or interactive writing. Read the message together, pointing to letters, words, and spaces.

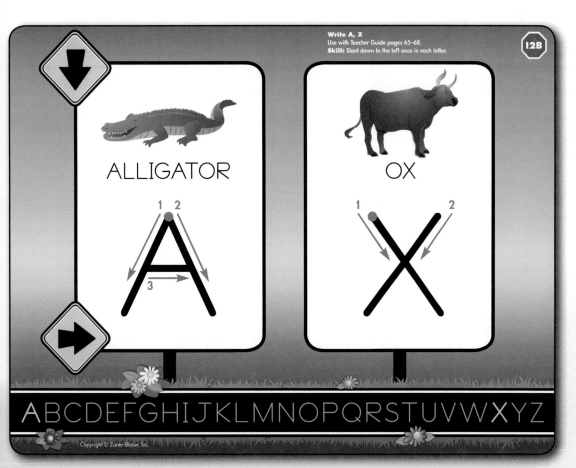

Write A, X
Use with Teacher Guide pages 65–68.
Skill: Slant down to the left once in each letter.

12B

ALLIGATOR

OX

ABCDEFGHIJKLMNOPQRSTUVWXYZ

Copyright © Zaner-Bloser, Inc.

Chant

Use this chant to help children remember how to hold their crayon when they draw or write.

Hold Your Crayon

Crayon, crayon,
Do you want to write?
Jump in my fingers.
I won't hold you tight.

Lean on tall friend,
Pointer on top,
Rest on my thumb,
I won't let you drop.

Ring and pinky
Tuck in beside.
They touch the paper
As we take a ride.

2 Center Time Days 3–5

*Choose multisensory activities for writing practice from the **Center Time** information on pages 18–19 or the activity below.*

Textured Letters Provide textured materials for children to place under blank paper as they write **A** and **X** with crayons. Try sandpaper, burlap, felt, and plastic cross-stitch canvas. Children may refer to Alphabet Cards **A** and **X** for the correct starting place for each letter. After using several textures, ask, "Which one made a bumpy pattern like alligator skin? Which one made a soft, brushy pattern like ox fur?" Extend practice over a series of days to make sure children are writing **A** from top to bottom. Also check that they can write **X** with the correct sequence: Slant right. Lift. Move the crayon to the top right. Slant left.

3 Play Time Days 3–5

*Use the **Play Time** information on page 20 and the idea below to introduce purposeful writing into children's dramatic play.*

Alphabet Restaurant Use shared/interactive writing on chart paper to list a food that begins with each letter of the alphabet: **apple, bacon, corn…zucchini**. Write the completed list on smaller paper and duplicate. Explain that this will be the menu at the Alphabet Restaurant. Set up the restaurant with tables, dishes, cooks, servers, and customers. Provide the menus as well as order pads, recipe cards, and paper for checks. Customers can order by reading letters and words from the menu.

Music, Mazes & More CD-ROM

Music for Movement
Sky-Writing (Track 1)
Wake Up Fingers (Track 4)
Hold Your Crayon (Track 8)
Slant Dance (Track 12)

Optional Practice Pages
You may wish to use some of these practice pages in the writing center.

Mazes: Pages 4, 8
Picture/Letter Cards: Pages 13–16
Letters: Pages 31, 54

Fun With Fundamentals

See pages 10–13 for more information about the development of these essential prewriting skills.

Developing Gross-Motor Skills

Write **A, X,** and other familiar letters on cards and tape them to orange playground cones. Let the cones mark activity stations on the playground. At each station, children do a physical activity related to the letter, such as running like an astronaut or throwing balls in a box.

Developing Fine-Motor Skills

Completing mazes teaches control of the writing tool and strengthens the ability of the eyes to work together. Print the mazes from the *Music, Mazes & More* CD-ROM and make them available in the writing center. Let children "rainbow write" by completing the same maze several times with a variety of crayon colors.

Developing Letter Recognition

Bury Letter Magnets in the sand table. Let children move magnets over the sand to see what is revealed. When children find and identify two letters, ask them to examine the shapes and tell what they have in common. Are they made up of the same kinds of lines?

Developing Print Awareness

Write on sentence strips: My favorite animals are ___. Help each child complete the sentence using invented spelling, shared writing, or dictation. Tape the strips down the length of a sheet of chart paper. Read together, sweeping the pointer finger left-to-right and back to the left to begin the next strip. Let children practice finger sweeping, too.

Developing Handwriting Skills

Left-Handed Writers Children who definitely have more strength and skill in the left hand should use that hand for writing. Left-handers may develop an awkward, hooked grasp in an effort to see what they are writing. Discourage this posture by having children write with small bits of chalk or crayon on a chalkboard or easel. Holding the crayon slightly farther back from the tip will help, too.

Featured Letters

Y Z

Objectives
- Recognize the letters **Y, Z**
- Write slant left lines
- Write the letters **Y, Z**
- Listen to a story
- Develop oral language and writing skills

Kit Materials
- Group Time Card 13
- *Music, Mazes & More* CD-ROM
- Alphabet Cards **Y, Z**
- Magnetic Letters and Board
- Touch and Trace Letter Cards **Y, Z**
- Wikki Stix®

Classroom Materials
- Old glove, thumbtacks, string
- Yo-yo
- Six zippers
- Two foam core or wood boards
- Hot glue gun, markers
- Pretend toy store supplies
- Clothesline, spring-type clothespins
- Snap-type plastic beads
- Paper circles, yarn
- Chalkboards, chalk

Stroke Focus

Slant left.

Letter Focus

1. Slant right.
2. Slant left.
   Pull down.

1. Slide.
   Slant left.
   Slide.

Teacher Tips
This lesson continues an emphasis on slant left lines, which are written from top right to bottom left. Because this slant line violates the left-to-right rule, it may be difficult for children to find its starting position and to write it in the correct direction. To help, focus children's attention on **Z**. Its distinctive shape and last-in-the-alphabet position make it easy to remember. If children begin **Z** correctly (with a slide to the right), they are almost guaranteed to write the center slant left line correctly.

Though it may seem more difficult than using a down-and-up motion, teach children to begin each of **Y**'s slant lines at the top. This will slow children down, preventing them from writing a messy **Y** and making the top of the letter too cramped.

Stroke Story

Children act out motions shown in red.

Prepare a yo-yo prop by fastening an old glove to the wall with thumbtacks, fingers facing left. Fasten a length of string to the pointer finger and staple a paper circle yo-yo to the bottom of the string. Also have a real yo-yo on hand.

Zebra got a new toy—a yo-yo! She carried it around with her all day, trying to throw it out, make it spin, and travel back up the string to her hand. It was harder than it looked!

When she slowly dropped the string down straight, the yo-yo just fell toward the floor and stayed there. (Several volunteers use the yo-yo prop to show the string hanging straight down.)

When she let the string slide straight out to the side, the yo-yo fell down, too. (Several volunteers make the string horizontal, then make it fall down.)

After lots of practice, Zebra could slant the yo-yo down toward the ground very quickly. Then, it would spin and travel back up the string. (Several volunteers slant the string down to the left. Let all children trace the slanted string from top to bottom.)

Zebra could make the yo-yo do a trick! She ran to show her family. (Let children try the real yo-yo.)

70

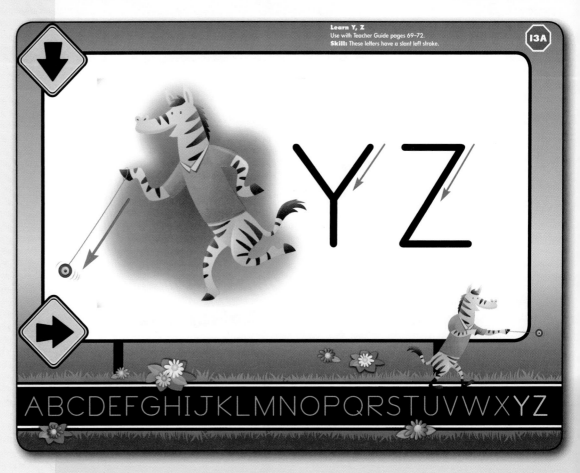

Learn Y, Z
Use with Teacher Guide pages 69–72.
Skill: These letters have a slant left stroke.

13A

Y Z

A B C D E F G H I J K L M N O P Q R S T U V W X Y Z

Group Time Days 1–2

*Gather children on the rug for group time. Use the notes below and the **Group Time** information found on pp. 16–17.*

Group Time Card 13A

1. Warm up with a song. Choose one listed at right.
2. Tell the Stroke Story.
3. Trace the arrow beside the yo-yo string from top to bottom. Say "slant left."
4. Sing "ABC Rap." Point to the target letters in yellow on the Alphabet Road.
5. Sky-write slant left lines in **Y** and **Z**. For each, say "slant left."

Group Time Card 13B

1. Warm up with a song. Choose one listed at right.
2. Sing "ABC Rap." Point to the letters on the Alphabet Road. Clap when you come to **Y** and **Z**.

3. Talk about the letter shapes. **Y** looks like a cone on a stick—you could hold **Y**'s stick and try to catch a ball inside. **Z** is the same upside-down. Who has these letters in his or her name? Read the word for each letter. Find the letter in the word.
4. Sky-write each letter several times, beginning at the green dot and following the arrows. Say the name of each line aloud.
5. Write an uppercase message, such as ZEBRA'S YO-YO ZOOMS, using shared or interactive writing. Read the message together, pointing to letters, words, and spaces.

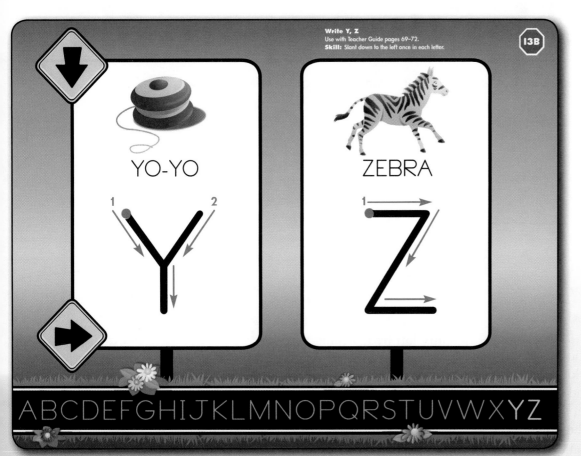

Write Y, Z
Use with Teacher Guide pages 69–72.
Skill: Slant down to the left once in each letter.

13B

YO-YO

ZEBRA

A B C D E F G H I J K L M N O P Q R S T U V W X Y Z

Chant

Use this chant with uppercase or lowercase alphabet cards to help children with letter recognition.

I Spy a Letter

I spy a letter.
Can you see?
It might be A.
It could be Z.
Here's a clue:
It looks like _____.
Here's a clue:
It sounds like _____.
Can you guess it?
It's a letter you've met.
It's part of
The alphabet!

2 Center Time Days 3–5

*Choose multisensory activities for writing practice from the **Center Time** information on pages 18–19 or the activity below.*

Zipper Letters Purchase six zippers from a fabric store. Arrange three zippers in the shape of **Y** on a piece of foam core board or wood. Arrange three zippers in a **Z** shape on another board. Make sure each zipper can be unzipped in the correct direction for each letter stroke. Then mount the zipper edges using hot glue. Use a marker to add green dots and arrows to show each letter's start and correct sequence. Let children unzip the letters, saying the name of each line aloud.

3 Play Time Days 3–5

*Use the **Play Time** information on page 20 and the idea below to introduce purposeful writing into children's dramatic play.*

Toy Store Gather toys from your classroom into one area and make a toy store. Provide a variety of labels, sticky notes, and other writing materials for making price tags and UPC codes, product labels, and a store sign. Let children make pretend money and bank cards to be used in a toy cash register or imaginary cash register. Roles include cashiers, stockers, sales people, customers, and product inventors who make new toys.

Music, Mazes & More CD-ROM

Music for Movement
ABC Rap (Track 2)
Thumbs Up (Track 5)
Slide Along (Track 10)
Slant Dance (Track 12)

Optional Practice Pages
You may wish to use some of these practice pages in the writing center.

Mazes: Pages 4, 8
Picture/Letter Cards: Pages 14, 16
Letters: Pages 55, 56

71

Fun With Fundamentals

See pages 10–13 for more information about the development of these essential prewriting skills.

Developing Fine-Motor Skills

String up a low clothesline in your classroom. Place Letter Magnets in a bowl. Show how to squeeze spring-type clothespins between the thumb and pointer finger of the dominant hand to pick up letters from the bowl and then hang them on the clothesline with assistance from the helper hand. Hang more letters to spell names and words. Can children pinch clothespins together to make the shapes of **Y** and **Z**?

Developing Spatial Awareness

Letters in this lesson slant down to the left. Help children identify left by fastening a small snap-type plastic bead on each child's left shoelace. Throughout the day, ask children to point to the left, jump to the left, raise their left hand, etc.

Developing Letter Recognition

Make yo-yos by stapling paper circles to long lengths of yarn. Write **Y, Z** or another familiar letter on each circle. Put the yo-yos in a messy pile on the floor. Ask each child to choose a string, pull on it to retrieve a yo-yo, and say the letter name.

Developing Sound-Symbol Awareness

Prop up Alphabet Cards beside objects in the room whose names match the letter's sound. For example, place the **B** card beside the books. Call on volunteers to find a card, name the letter, and guess the object name that matches the letter's sound.

Developing Handwriting Skills

For writing instruction, chalkboards have an advantage over marker boards in the preschool classroom. Chalk may be broken into small bits that must be pinched between the fingers, ensuring good hand position. The friction of chalk against the chalkboard slows children's writing and provides good sensory feedback. By contrast, slick marker boards encourage quick writing. While marker boards may help with a sense of "flow" in writing, they do not aid careful letter formation.

Featured Letters

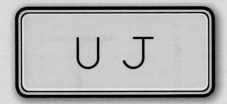

Objectives
- Recognize the letters **U, J**
- Write curve lines
- Write the letters **U, J**
- Listen to a story
- Develop oral language and writing skills

Kit Materials
- Group Time Card 14
- *Music, Mazes & More* CD-ROM
- Alphabet Cards **U, J**
- Magnetic Letters and Board
- Touch and Trace Letter Cards **U, J**
- Wikki Stix®

Classroom Materials
- Blank drawing paper, crayons, gummy worms, glue
- Pretend flower shop supplies
- Commercial or homemade ball scoops and soft balls
- Construction paper, tissue paper, scissors, glue
- Sand table, shovels
- Wood puzzle pieces, paper, crayons

Stroke Focus

Curve forward.

Curve back.

Letter Focus

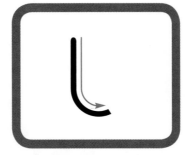

1. Curve forward.

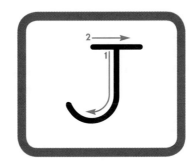

1. Curve back.
2. Slide.

Teacher Tips

The letter **J** is frequently reversed by young children. This is due, in part, to **J**'s rule-breaking formation—its body begins at right and curves left. The problem of reversals, however, is more generally caused by children's inexperience with the world of print and the new task of writing specific letter shapes. Reversals are common well into the elementary school years, and should not be a cause of concern for teachers of young children. Mastery will come with time and experience.

Some children learn mirror-like pairs (such as **U** and **J**) more easily when the letters are presented and practiced on separate days or weeks. Other children benefit from examining the confusing letters together. You may wish to try both strategies.

Here, **U** and **J** are paired with a focus on writing curves. Praise children for writing smooth curves in both directions. Help with directionality by drawing green dots to show where **U** and **J** begin and red dots to show where they should end.

Most people prefer the way **J** looks with a slide-stroke "cap" on top. Explain that **J**'s cap helps it balance so that it doesn't roll on the curved base.

Stroke Story

Children act out motions shown in red.

Jaguar and his mother went to the store and bought flowers in pots. They bought a big trowel for Mother and a small trowel for Jaguar. Now it was time to plant the flowers.

Mother dug a hole for each flower. She pressed her trowel deep in the ground and scooped out the soil again and again. (With writing hand, hold pretend trowel and make complete, U-shaped scooping motion to the right. Repeat.) She gently pulled each plant from its pot, settled it in the hole, and patted dirt all around. (Act out planting several flowers.)

Jaguar played in the dirt. He pressed his trowel into the ground, but he didn't scoop the soil out. Instead, he curved his trowel up so he could see what was in the dirt. (With writing hand, hold pretend trowel and make incomplete scooping motion to the left that stops short in a hook- or J-shape. Repeat.) Jaguar saw something slick and wiggly. It was an earthworm! He pulled it out and it curved on his paw. (Handle pretend worm.) Jaguar knew that earthworms were good for plants. He put his friend back in the dirt beside a flower.

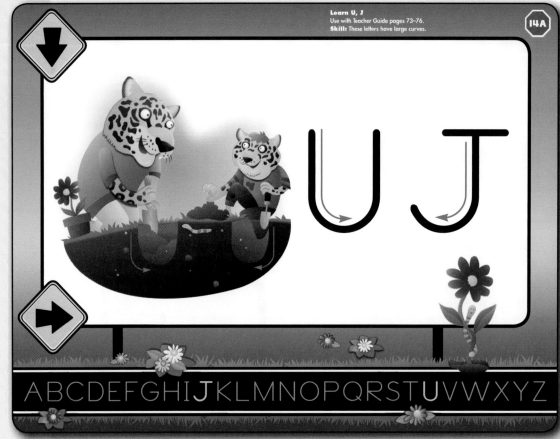

Learn U, J
Use with Teacher Guide pages 73–76.
Skill: These letters have large curves.

14A

ABCDEFGHI**J**KLMNOPQRST**U**VWXYZ

Group Time Days 1–2

*Gather children together for group time. Use the **Group Time** information on pp. 16–17 and the notes below.*

Group Time Card 14A
1. Warm up with a song. Choose one listed at right.
2. Tell the Stroke Story.
3. Trace the arrow near the mother's trowel. Say "curve forward." Trace the arrow near the child's trowel. Say "curve back."
4. Sing "ABC Rap." Point to the target letters in yellow on the Alphabet Road.
5. Sky-write the curve in **U** and say "curve forward." Sky-write the curve in **J** and say "curve back."

Group Time Card 14B
1. Warm up with a song. Choose one listed at right.

2. Sing "ABC Rap." Point to the letters on the Alphabet Road. Clap when you come to **U** and **J**.
3. Talk about letter shapes. **U** is a hole you could fill up with dirt. Folded in half, **U**'s sides are the same. **J** is a fish hook. It wears a hat. Who has these letters in his or her name? Read the word for each letter. Find the letter in the word.
4. Sky-write each letter several times, beginning at the green dot and following the arrows.
5. Write an uppercase message, such as JAGUAR'S WORM JIGGLES UNDERGROUND, using shared or interactive writing. Read the message together, pointing to letters, words, and spaces.

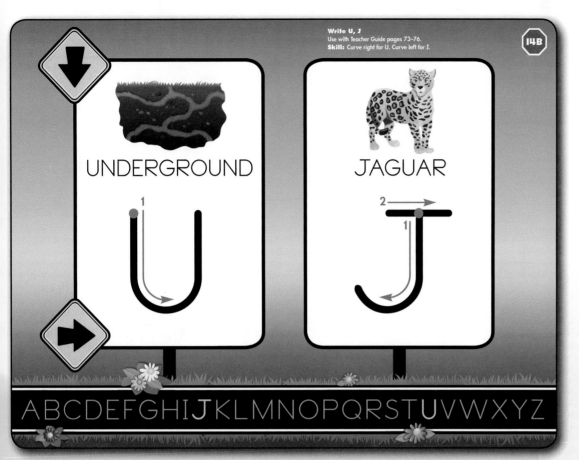

Write U, J
Use with Teacher Guide pages 73–76.
Skill: Curve right for U. Curve left for J.

14B

UNDERGROUND

JAGUAR

ABCDEFGHIJKLMNOPQRSTUVWXYZ

Chant

Use this chant to help children remember to use the helper hand when they draw or write.

Helper Hand

Helper hand, helper hand,
Help me write.
Stay flat and hold my paper
As we move from left to right.

Music, Mazes & More
CD-ROM

Music for Movement
ABC Rap (Track 2)
Thumbkin (Track 6)
My Two Hands (Track 8)
Slide Along (Track 10)

Optional Practice Pages
You may wish to use some of these practice pages in the writing center.

Mazes: Pages 6, 10, 12
Picture/Letter Cards: Pages 13–16
Letters: Pages 40, 51

2 Center Time Days 3–5

Choose multisensory activities for writing practice from the **Center Time** information on pages 18–19 or the activity below.

Letter Worms Show how to crayon a long slide line across a sheet of drawing paper to be the ground. Underground, draw dirt and tunnels. Above ground, draw something that begins with **J**, such as a jaguar, a jet, or a juggler. Distribute gummy worms and glue. Help children glue one worm in a **U** shape underground and one worm in a **J** shape above ground. They may need to break a worm to form **J**'s slide line. That's okay—earthworms regenerate when they lose body segments! Children can trace the gummy letters in the correct direction, saying the name of each line.

3 Play Time Days 3–5

Use the **Play Time** information on page 20 and the idea below to introduce purposeful writing into children's dramatic play.

ABC Flower Shop Provide silk flowers or make flowers with drinking straw stems and construction paper faces. Write an uppercase letter on each flower. Then set up a flower shop. Include paper cups for making flower arrangements. Customers may order flowers according to letters, or order arrangements that spell out names or words. Have writing materials on hand for taking phone orders, creating signs, and making pretend money and bank cards.

75

Fun With Fundamentals

See pages 10–13 for more information about the development of these essential prewriting skills.

Developing Gross-Motor Skills

Provide commercial ball scoops or make them by cutting used milk jugs with a utility knife. Have children hold the scoop handle with the writing hand. Show pairs how to toss and catch soft balls by swinging the scoops in a wide curve.

Developing Fine-Motor Skills

Give children's hands a fine-motor workout as they make an underground/above ground collage with paper and glue. Have them tear brown paper for dirt, use scissors to cut a strip of green paper into fringe for grass, and roll tissue paper into balls for clouds, flowers, etc.

Developing Spatial Awareness

Attach Letter Magnet **L** to the left side of the sand table and Letter Magnet **R** to the right. Provide shovels for 2 to 4 children and have them stand side-by-side at the table. Then ask them to scoop sand to the left or right. Repeat, substituting "forward" for "right" and "back" for "left." Finally, ask them to form **U** and **J** shapes in the sand, following the correct stroke sequence/direction for each letter.

Developing Letter Recognition

Ask children to sit on the floor. Give each child 3 to 4 Wikki Stix pieces. Then call out a letter. Children use the pieces to form the uppercase letter on the floor. Choose a child who has formed the letter correctly to be the next to call out a letter. Praise children for forming individual lines correctly as well as complete letters.

Developing Handwriting Skills

Build children's ability to control a writing tool by having them use wood puzzle pieces as stencils. The helper hand should hold the puzzle piece still as children trace around its shape with a crayon. Play music and have children stop their crayons when the music stops.

Featured Letters

Objectives
- Recognize the letters **l, i, u**
- Write pull down lines
- Write the letters **l, i, u**
- Listen to a story
- Develop oral language and writing skills

Kit Materials
- Group Time Card 15
- *Music, Mazes & More* CD-ROM
- Alphabet Cards **l, i, u**
- Magnetic Letters and Board
- Touch and Trace Letter Cards **l, i, u**
- Wikki Stix®
- Blank Story Journal

Classroom Materials
- Blank paper, crayons
- Supplies for a pretend weather station
- Drawing paper, washable markers, spray bottles
- Umbrella, large leaf, ruler
- Toy cars

Stroke Focus

Pull down.

Letter Focus

1. Pull down.

1. Pull down.
2. Dot.

1. Curve forward. Pull down.

Teacher Tips

Before they begin to write lowercase letters, children should demonstrate the ability to:

- write basic strokes (pull down lines, slide lines, circle lines, slant lines) with ease;
- recognize and write many uppercase letters; and
- use a three-finger grasp with a clearly established dominant hand

Children who have not demonstrated these skills will benefit from continued practice with uppercase letters. In fact, mastery of uppercase letters alone provides an excellent foundation for success in kindergarten.

Zaner-Bloser's Continuous Stroke Alphabet is designed to require as few crayon-lifts as possible. Letters are formed efficiently from smooth, continuous strokes. For this reason, several lowercase letters contain retraced lines. Lowercase **u** is one example. As they write the final pull down line in **u**, children must retrace the right side of the initial curve. Emphasize the importance of retracing or "driving on the same line," slowly and carefully to avoid double lines. When children spot a letter with a retrace, teach them to make a "beep, beep" sound (like a truck backing up) to signal caution.

Stroke Story

Children act out motions shown in red.

Before the rain storm started, Lion took his rain gauge outside and set it on the driveway. Rain would fall into the tube so Lion could measure it. Back inside, Lion watched out the window as it started to rain.

The raindrops came slowly at first, then fell faster and faster. (Use ten fingers to show raindrops falling slow, then fast.) Lightning lit up the sky and thunder clapped. (Clap for thunder.) Wind blew leaves down from the trees. (Lower outstretched hands to show leaves falling down.) For a few minutes, the rain turned to hail. The ice balls fell down to the ground, then bounced up and fell down again. (Use pointer finger to show hail fall, bounce up, and fall again.)

Finally, the sky got brighter. The rain slowed down. Lion put on his raincoat and boots, got his umbrella, and went outside. He jumped up and splashed down into a puddle. (Jump up and down.) Lion reached down to pick up the rain gauge. There was water inside. Almost one inch!

When he was done playing, Lion came in and pulled the zipper on his raincoat down. (Pull pretend zipper down.) "Dad," he yelled. "May I please have some hot chocolate?"

Learn l, i, u
Use with Teacher Guide pages 77–80.
Skill: These letters have pull down lines.

15A

l i u

a b c d e f g h i j k l m n o p q r s t u v w x y z

Group Time Days 1–2

*Gather children together for group time. Use the **Group Time** information on pp. 16–17 and the notes below.*

Group Time Card 15A

1. Warm up with a song. Choose one listed at right.
2. Tell the Stroke Story.
3. Trace the arrow beside the zipper from top to bottom. Say "pull down."
4. Sing "ABC Rap." Point to the target letters in yellow on the Alphabet Road.
5. Sky-write pull down lines in **l, i,** and **u**. For each, say "pull down."

Group Time Card 15B

1. Warm up with a song. Choose one listed at right.
2. Sing "ABC Rap." Point to the letters on the Alphabet Road. Clap when you come to **l, i,** and **u**.

3. Talk about letter shapes. The letter **l** is a lollipop stick and **i** throws a ball (dot) over its head. Lowercase **u** is the same as uppercase **U**, but with a pull down line at the end. Read the word for each letter. Find the letter in the word. Who has these letters in his or her name?
4. Sky-write each letter several times, beginning at the green dot and following the arrows. Say the name of each line aloud.
5. Write a message, such as "Lion jumps in puddles," using shared or interactive writing. Point to letters, words, and spaces.

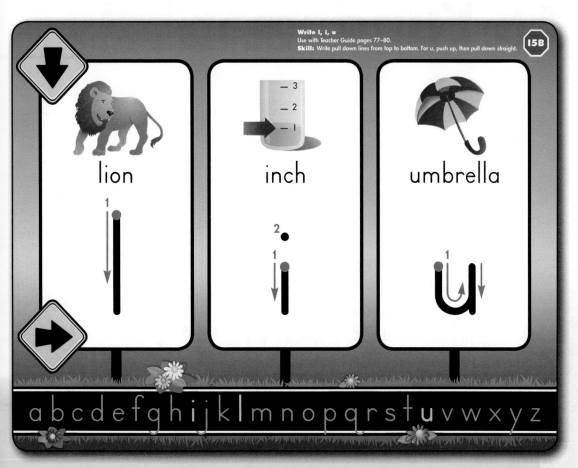

Write l, i, u
Use with Teacher Guide pages 77–80.
Skill: Write pull down lines from top to bottom. For u, push up, then pull down straight.

15B

lion

inch

umbrella

a b c d e f g h i j k l m n o p q r s t u v w x y z

Chant
Use this chant to help children remember how to hold their crayon when they draw or write

Hold Your Crayon
Crayon, crayon,
Do you want to write?
Jump in my fingers.
I won't hold you tight.

Lean on tall friend,
Pointer on top,
Rest on my thumb,
I won't let you drop.

Ring and pinky
Tuck in beside.
They touch the paper
As we take a ride.

2 Center Time Days 3–5

Choose multisensory activities for writing practice from the **Center Time** *information on pages 18–19 or the activity below.*

Touch and Trace Supply Touch and Trace Letter Cards **Ll, Ii,** and **Tt,** blank paper, and crayons. Show how to trace lowercase and uppercase letters with the pointer finger of the writing hand as the helper hand secures the card. Start each letter at the arrow, tracing lines in the correct sequence. As they trace, children should say the name of each line. They can then use paper and crayons to make letter rubbings. Children may color each pull down line blue to look like a raindrop.

3 Play Time Days 3–5

Use the **Play Time** *information on page 20 and the idea below to introduce purposeful writing into children's dramatic play.*

Weather Station Set up a weather station near a window in your classroom. Provide books and posters about weather, a large map and pointer, a thermometer, and a rain gauge or ruler. Ask children to observe weather conditions and record their observations in notebooks and on charts. Ask them to prepare and deliver a weather report for the television news. You may wish to make a video tape of the performance.

Music, Mazes & More CD-ROM

Music for Movement
ABC Rap (Track 2)
Wake Up Fingers (Track 4)
Hold Your Crayon (Track 8)
I Pull Down (Track 9)

Optional Practice Pages
You may wish to use some of these practice pages in the writing center.

Mazes: Pages 1, 2, 5, 6, 9, 10, 12
Picture/Letter Cards: Pages 13–18
Letters: Pages 65, 68, 77

Fun With Fundamentals

See pages 10–13 for more information about the development of these essential prewriting skills.

Developing Fine-Motor Skills

Have children draw outdoor scenes with washable markers on drawing paper. Lay the completed pictures outside on the ground. Then provide several spray bottles filled with water. Children can take turns using the sprayers to make it "rain" on the scenes and watching the colors run. Squeezing the spray trigger builds hand strength.

Developing Print Awareness

Make a silly weather book. On the first page, write "Today we had the craziest weather ever." For each page that follows, help a child complete the sentence "_____ fell from the sky." Children may use invented spelling, shared writing, or teacher dictation to complete their page according to their ability level. Let children illustrate their pages. Bind the book and read it together.

Developing Letter Recognition

Display Alphabet Cards for uppercase **L, I**, and **U**. Put lowercase Letter Magnets in a bowl nearby. Ask children to match the lowercase magnets to the uppercase letters, turning the cards over to self-check.

Developing Sound-Symbol Awareness

In an open area, place three items at a distance from each other: an umbrella, a ruler, and a large leaf. Say "umbrella," "inch," and "leaf," emphasizing each beginning sound. Then say words such as *lion, underground, ladder, igloo, ink,* and *umpire.* For each word, children should scramble to stand next to the item that matches the beginning sound.

Developing Handwriting Skills

Retraces Letters with retraced lines, including **u**, may be challenging for young writers. Let children trace large letter models, such as those on Group Time Cards or Alphabet Cards, with toy cars. For retraced lines, cars must turn around and "drive on the same road" again.

80

Featured Letters

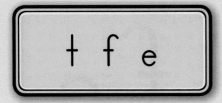

Objectives
- Recognize the letters **t, f, e**
- Write slide lines
- Write the letters **t, f, e**
- Listen to a story
- Develop oral language and writing skills

Kit Materials
- Group Time Card 16
- *Music, Mazes & More* CD-ROM
- Alphabet Cards **t, f, e**
- Magnetic Letters and Board
- Touch and Trace Letter Cards **t, f, e**
- Wikki Stix®

Classroom Materials
- Shallow trays or shoebox lids
- Sand or salt, washable markers
- Supplies for a pretend grocery store
- Play dough and tools
- Red yarn
- Blanket, toys or classroom objects
- Plastic bowls

Stroke Focus

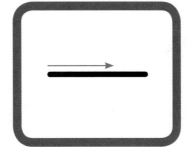

Slide.

Letter Focus

1. Pull down.
2. Slide.

1. Curve back.
   Pull down.
2. Slide.

1. Slide.
   Circle back.

Teacher Tips

Even as children learn to distinguish "big" (uppercase) letters from "small" (lowercase) letters, the actual size at which they write the two kinds of letters may not differ much at all. This should not be a cause for concern. Children will learn to adjust the size of their writing in later years. For now, writing all letters at a large size on unlined paper is best.

Because **f**'s initial curve breaks the left-to-right rule, give children some extra help in getting it started in the correct direction. Mark a green dot where it begins and include a counterclockwise arrow.

After children learn lowercase **e**, they will enjoy writing the straight-then-curved letter. Mark a green dot for its beginning and tell children to make sure they touch the dot again as they circle back.

Stroke Story

Children act out motions shown in red.

Turtle has a hard shell to cover and protect him, four strong legs, and a long, bendable neck. When Turtle plays, he likes to move his body in lots of different ways.

He can swim in the pond just as well as any fish. (Lay on belly; move arms and legs in swimming motions.)

When his belly gets stuck in the mud, he can use his legs to turn in a circle. (Still on belly, move arms and legs to turn in a circle.)

When he plays hide-and-seek, he can tuck all his legs and his head right inside his shell. Sometimes, he turns over and rolls on his shell like an egg. (Lay on back, tucking arms, legs, and head, and roll on back.)

But Turtle likes it best when it is playtime at his school. Then his short legs come out of his shell. He finds his favorite dump truck and loads it with toys. He likes to push the truck and make its wheels slide smoothly along the floor. His short turtle legs slide slowly across the floor, too. Then he feels very happy. (Turn to the right and walk slowly on hands and knees across the floor.)

Learn **t, f, e**
Use with Teacher Guide pages 81–84.
Skill: These letters have slide lines.

16A

Group Time Days 1–2

*Gather children together for group time. Use the **Group Time** information on pp. 16–17 and the notes below.*

Group Time Card 16A
1. Warm up with a song. Choose one listed at right.
2. Tell the Stroke Story.
3. Trace the arrow beside the dump truck. Say "slide."
4. Sing "ABC Rap." Point to the target letters in yellow on the Alphabet Road.
5. Sky-write slide lines in **t, f,** and **e**. For each, say "slide."

Group Time Card 16B
1. Warm up with a song. Choose one listed at right.
2. Sing "ABC Rap." Point to the letters on the Alphabet Road. Clap when you come to **t, f,** and **e**.

3. Talk about letter shapes. Lowercase **f** is a tall **t** that droops at the top; **e**'s top looks like an eyelid. Who has these letters in his or her name? Can these letters be found in the room? Read the word for each letter. Find the letter in the word.
4. Sky-write each letter several times, beginning at the green dot and following the arrows. Say the name of each line aloud.
5. Write a message, such as "Turtle found his favorite truck," using shared or interactive writing. Read the message together, pointing to letters, words, and spaces.

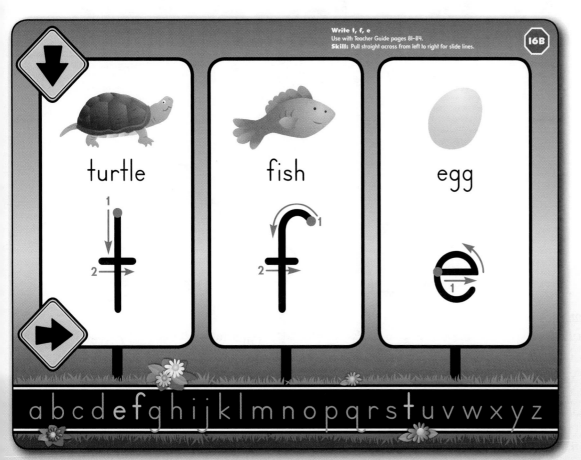

turtle

fish

egg

Write t, f, e
Use with Teacher Guide pages 81–84.
Skill: Pull straight across from left to right for slide lines.

16B

a b c d **e** f g h i j k l m n o p q r s **t** u v w x y z

Chant
Use this chant to remind children how to write in the sky.

Sky-Writing
I draw a paper in the sky.
I hold two fingers way up high.
I draw big lines and letters, too.
I'm sky-writing—so can you!

---

2 Center Time Days 3–5

*Choose multisensory activities for writing practice from the **Center Time** information on pages 18–19 or the activity below.*

Turtle in the Sand Fill shallow trays or shoebox lids with sand or salt. Tell children their writing hand will be a turtle. The fist is a turtle in its shell. The pointer fingers stretches out to be the head. (Use washable markers to draw turtle features on children's hands.) Say the name of each line as the turtle writes **t, f,** and **e** in the sand. Make up a story to fit the formation of each letter. (Example: For **e,** Turtle first slides from the center of the pond, then circles around the pond until he stops and finds a flower to munch.)

3 Play Time Days 3–5

*Use the **Play Time** information on page 20 and the idea below to introduce purposeful writing into children's dramatic play.*

Grocery Store Set up a grocery store in the housekeeping center. Bring in a variety of clean, empty food containers and plain containers for children to label. Provide writing materials for shopping lists, price tags, coupons, signs, pretend money, bank cards, and receipts. Also have grocery ads available for children to read and examine. Children's roles may include farmer, delivery truck driver, store stocker, cashier, and customer.

Music, Mazes & More CD-ROM

Music for Movement
Sky-Writing (Track 1)
Top to Bottom (Track 3)
Thumbs Up (Track 5)
Slide Along (Track 10)

Optional Practice Pages
You may wish to use some of these practice pages in the writing center.

Mazes: Pages 1, 2, 5, 6, 9, 10, 12
Picture/Letter Cards: Pages 13–18
Letters: Pages 61, 62, 76

Fun With Fundamentals

See pages 10–13 for more information about the development of these essential prewriting skills.

Developing Fine-Motor Skills

Working with play dough is an excellent way to strengthen and develop the hands. Roll dough into meatball-sized balls between the palms (to develop hand arches) or into pea-sized balls between the pads of the thumb and pointer finger (to refine motor separation in the hand).

More ways to develop the arches: Roll dough with a rolling pin, keeping the hands open on the pin instead of using the handles. Slice dough "snakes" into segments with a pizza wheel or plastic knife held with the pointer finger on top of the tool to provide forward and downward pressure.

Developing Spatial Awareness

Tie short lengths of red yarn in loops to make rings or bracelets for children to wear on their right hands. Let children wear them for short periods while you ask them to "raise their right hand, touch their left foot, point to the right side of the room," etc.

Developing Print Awareness

On a tabletop, line up 3–6 toys or classroom objects. Cover them with a blanket. Gather children, then lift the blanket and name each item in left-to-right order. Cover the objects again. Can children remember the items in order from left to right? On the chalkboard, write the object names and read them from left to right.

Developing Letter Recognition

Distribute "turtle shells" (plastic bowls) and let children choose a Letter Magnet to hide underneath. Each child can then give clues about his or her letter (such as what kinds of lines it contains, where it is found in the alphabet, and whose names include it). Can children guess the letter?

Developing Sound-Symbol Awareness

Using shared/interactive writing, write tongue twisters about Tim Turtle or Fiona Fish on chart paper. Have volunteers circle or highlight each **T, t, F,** or **f.** Repeat the tongue twisters together, picking up speed each time.

Featured Letters

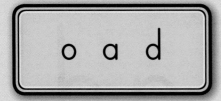

Objectives
- Recognize the letters **o, a, d**
- Write circle back lines
- Write the letters **o, a, d**
- Listen to a story
- Develop oral language and writing skills

Kit Materials
- Group Time Card 17
- *Music, Mazes & More* CD-ROM
- Alphabet Cards **o, a, d**
- Magnetic Letters and Board
- Touch and Trace Letter Cards **o, a, d**
- Wikki Stix®

Classroom Materials
- Drawing paper, white glue, gelatin powder, cotton swabs
- Clothesline, spring-type clothespins
- Small screwdrivers and screws
- Toy cars

Stroke Focus

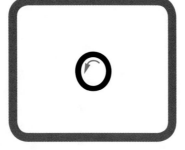

Circle back.

Letter Focus

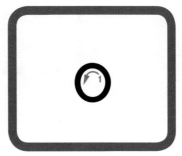

1. Circle back.

1. Circle back.
   Push up.
   Pull down.

1. Circle back.
   Push up.
   Pull down.

Teacher Tips

The letters in this lesson all begin by circling back (counterclockwise) from the same starting position, about 1:00 on a clock face.

The benefits of starting **d** with a circle will become apparent later, when children learn to write **b**. Lowercase **d** and **b** are the letters most commonly confused by young writers. It helps very much to have the habit of beginning **d** with a circle back line (like **o** and **a**) and beginning **b** at a completely different place—at the top, with a pull down line. Show children that **d** is just like **a**, only taller.

Both **a** and **d** require a retrace. After the circle, the writer pushes up, then pulls down, following the same line. Provide ample time to practice these formations slowly and carefully, avoiding double lines. Children who have difficulty may prefer the lift method, described on page 88.

Stroke Story

Children act out motions shown in red.

Otter loved to roll. It was her favorite thing to do. She tucked her head, bent her knees, pushed against the floor with her toes, and circled away. (Somersault to the left.)

On Sunday, Otter rolled in the grass. That left green marks on her clothes. (Somersault to the left.)

On Monday, Otter rolled in the kitchen. She got yogurt on her clothes. (Somersault to the left.)

On Tuesday, Otter rolled in the mud. You can imagine what THAT did to her clothes. (Somersault to the left.)

On Wednesday, Otter rolled into the art corner at school and got purple and pink paint on her clothes. (Somersault to the left.)

On Thursday, Otter rolled in the bathroom. Toothpaste squirted on her clothes AND on her. (Somersault to the left.)

On Friday, Otter rolled into her little sister's bottle of milk and…you know what happened. (Somersault to the left.)

On Saturday, Otter and Dad went to the Laundromat. Otter played with her toys and watched her clothes circle around and around in the washer and dryer. (Roll head around to the left.) "Dad," she said, "Rolling makes my clothes dirty. Should I stop rolling?"

"No," said Dad. "Your clothes will come clean. It makes you happy to roll. It makes me happy, too."

86

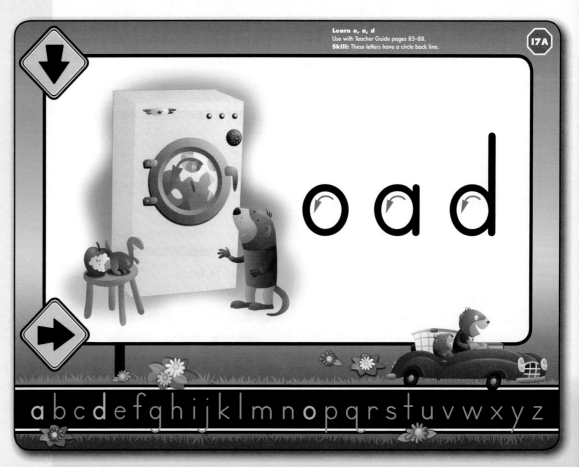

Learn o, a, d
Use with Teacher Guide pages 85–88.
Skill: These letters have a circle back line.

17A

o a d

a b c d e f g h i j k l m n o p q r s t u v w x y z

Group Time Days 1–2

*Gather children together for group time. Use the **Group Time** information on pp. 16–17 and the notes below.*

Group Time Card 17A
1. Warm up with a song. Choose one listed at right.
2. Tell the Stroke Story.
3. Trace the arrow on the machine. Say "circle back."
4. Sing "ABC Rap." Point to the target letters in yellow on the Alphabet Road.
5. Sky-write circle back lines in **o, a,** and **d.** For each, say "circle back."

Group Time Card 17B
1. Warm up with a song. Choose one listed at right.
2. Sing "ABC Rap." Point to the letters on the Alphabet Road. Clap when you come to **o, a,** and **d.**

3. Talk about letter shapes. They all have circles. Lowercase **o** can be seen in **a** and **d; a** can be seen in **d.** Who has these letters in his or her name? Can these letters be found in the room? Read the word for each letter. Find the letter in the word.
4. Sky-write each letter several times, beginning at the green dot and following the arrows. Say the name of each line aloud.
5. Write a message, such as "Otter rolled away," using shared or interactive writing. Read the message together, pointing to letters, words, and spaces.

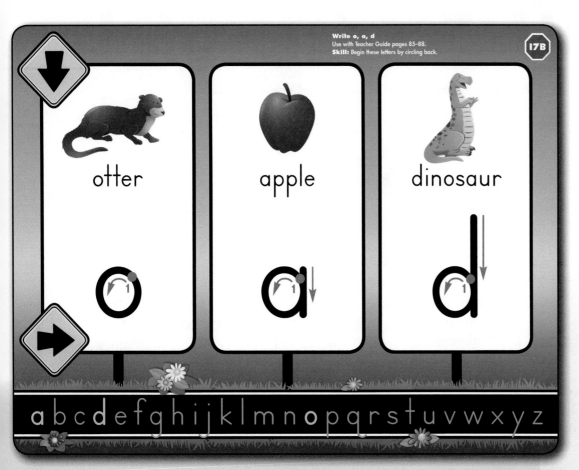

Write o, a, d
Use with Teacher Guide pages 85–88.
Skill: Begin these letters by circling back.

17B

otter

apple

dinosaur

a b c d e f g h i j k l m n o p q r s t u v w x y z

Chant
Use this chant with uppercase or lowercase alphabet cards to help children with letter recognition.

I Spy a Letter
I spy a letter.
Can you see?
It might be A.
It could be Z.
Here's a clue:
It looks like _____.
Here's a clue:
It sounds like _____.
Can you guess it?
It's a letter you've met.
It's part of
The alphabet!

2 Center Time Days 3–5

*Choose multisensory activities for writing practice from the **Center Time** information on pages 18–19 or the activity below.*

Smelly Letters Cut sheets of drawing paper into large t-shirt shapes. In a bowl, mix white glue with gelatin powder. Let children use cotton swabs to "get the shirts dirty" by painting the letters **o, a,** and **d** with the glue mixture. Children should say the name of each line as they paint. Remind children to retrace their lines carefully in **a** and **d**. When the letters are dry, they may be traced and sniffed.

3 Play Time Days 3–5

*Use the **Play Time** information on page 20 and the idea below to introduce purposeful writing into children's dramatic play.*

T-Shirts, Inc. Cut sheets of drawing paper into large t-shirt shapes. Talk about words that appear on t-shirts, including names of people, characters, and places as well as phrases such as "I love soccer." Let each child write on a paper shirt. Then string up a clothesline in the classroom. Write uppercase and lowercase letters on spring-type clothespins. Let children hang up their shirts, choosing clothespins that match letters on the shirts or that spell words.

Music, Mazes & More CD-ROM

Music for Movement
ABC Rap (Track 2)
Thumbkin (Track 6)
Hold Your Crayon (Track 8)
Circle Song (Track 11)

Optional Practice Pages
You may wish to use some of these practice pages in the writing center.

Mazes: Pages 1, 2, 3, 5, 7, 9, 11
Picture/Letter Cards: Pages 13–18
Letters: Pages 57, 60, 71

87

Fun With Fundamentals

See pages 10–13 for more information about the development of these essential prewriting skills.

Developing Gross-Motor Skills

In a dramatic movement exercise, have children act out the experience of being articles of clothing in a giant washing machine. "Toss" each child in the machine and set it spinning in a counterclockwise direction. Pretend to add soap bubbles as children sway about. Move the wet and limp "clothes" to the dryer, then fold and sort the clean laundry.

Developing Fine-Motor Skills

Using small screwdrivers—such as those that come with toy workbenches, Erector® sets, or other building sets—develops hand strength and controlled finger movements. Set up a center where children can work with these tools. Display large clockwise and counterclockwise arrows that encourage children to move the tools in both directions.

Developing Spatial Awareness

Have children play with toy cars or other vehicles on the floor or tabletop as you give direction-related commands. Say "drive to the right; drive to the left; circle back; make a U-turn" etc. Then give commands for "driving" specific letter shapes.

Developing Letter Recognition

From the *Music, Mazes & More* CD-ROM, print two copies of Practice Pages 29–30 (for lowercase matching) or one copy of Practice Pages 27–30 (for uppercase/lowercase matching). Cut the letter cards apart. Have pairs of children turn the cards facedown and play Memory. When they make a match, children cannot keep the cards until they name the letter shown and tell one kind of line it contains (pull down, slide, circle, slant).

Developing Handwriting Skills

Lift Method Children who have continued difficulty with retracing in **a** and **d** may benefit from lifting the crayon after the circle is completed and positioning it above and to the right of the circle to begin the pull down line. The "push up" step is eliminated. While this method has its own challenges—it can be difficult to judge where to begin the pull down line so that it touches the circle—it may be welcomed by a child who is frustrated with retracing.

Featured Letters

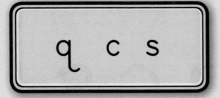

Objectives
- Recognize the letters **q, c, s**
- Write circle back and curve back lines
- Write the letters **q, c, s**
- Listen to a story
- Develop oral language and writing skills

Kit Materials
- Group Time Card 18
- *Music, Mazes & More* CD-ROM
- Alphabet Cards **q, c, s**
- Magnetic Letters and Board
- Touch and Trace Letter Cards **q, c, s**
- Wikki Stix®

Classroom Materials
- Soft balls or wads of paper
- Audiotape and player
- Variety of game supplies
- Balloons, permanent marker
- Scissors, small piece of sponge, paper
- Chart paper
- Block, thick paintbrush, or other object to measure spaces between words in text

Stroke Focus

Circle back.

Curve back.

Letter Focus

I. Circle back.
  Push up.
  Pull down.
  Curve forward.

I. Circle back.

I. Curve back.
  Curve forward.

Teacher Tips

As children begin to introduce lowercase letters into their own writing, don't be surprised if they mix uppercase and lowercase letters indiscriminately. This should not be a cause for concern. Encourage children's exploration of the new lowercase shapes and occasionally point out correct uses of uppercase letters in environmental print—at the beginning of names, in book titles, and on signs.

Explain that some lowercase letters have the exact same shape as their parents, only smaller. Look together at an alphabet chart (such as the one on Group Time Card *25*) and ask children to point out uppercase/lowercase pairs that have the same shape, including **Cc** and **Ss**. Ask them to point out pairs that have similar, but different, shapes.

Stroke Story

Children act out motions shown in red.

Cow and Duck wanted to play catch. Cow tossed the ball so it curved toward Duck. Duck tried to catch it, but the ball slipped through his wings. Cow picked up the ball and tossed it again. Again, Duck missed.

"I am short," said Duck sadly. "It's hard to reach my wings up to catch. Maybe we can't play together."

"No," said Cow. "We are friends. We'll think of a way. I know! You are short, but you can do something amazing. You can fly!"

"That's true," said Duck. "I can fly up and catch the ball when you throw it. Let's try!"

Cow and Duck played the new game. They had so much fun! Cow tossed the ball so it curved in the air. Then Duck flew up, caught the ball in his beak, and flew back around in a circle to return the ball to Cow. Duck even tried some fancy tricks, curving back and forward as he flew. "Quack," he called happily.

(Use soft balls or wads of paper. Playing in pairs, one child can toss the ball up and to the left while the other jumps up to catch it and completes the circle back motion to the tosser. Try an S-shape, too. Switch roles and play again.)

Learn **q, c, s**
Use with Teacher Guide pages 89–92.
Skill: These letters have a circle back or curve back line.

18A

a b c d e f g h i j k l m n o p q r s t u v w x y z

90

Group Time Days 1–2

*Gather children together for group time. Use the **Group Time** information on pages 16–17 and the notes below.*

Group Time Card 18A

1. Warm up with a song. Choose one listed at right.
2. Tell the Stroke Story.
3. Trace the arrow near the ball; make it a complete circle. Say, "circle back." Trace the arrow in a partial circle. Say "curve back."
4. Sing "ABC Rap." Point to the target letters in yellow on the Alphabet Road.
5. Sky-write the circle back lines in **q** and **c** and say "circle back." Sky-write the top curve in **s** and say "curve back."

Group Time Card 18B

1. Warm up with a song. Choose one listed at right.

2. Sing "ABC Rap." Point to the letters on the Alphabet Road. Clap when you come to **c, q,** and **s**.
3. Talk about letter shapes. The letter **q** has a tail that faces out; it won't catch the circle if it falls; **c** and **s** look just like their parents **C** and **S**. Who has these letters in his or her name? Read the word for each letter. Find the letter in the word.
4. Sky-write each letter several times, beginning at the green dot and following the arrows. Say the name of each line aloud.
5. Write a message, such as "Duck quacks and catches the ball," using shared or interactive writing. Read the message together, pointing to letters, words, and spaces.

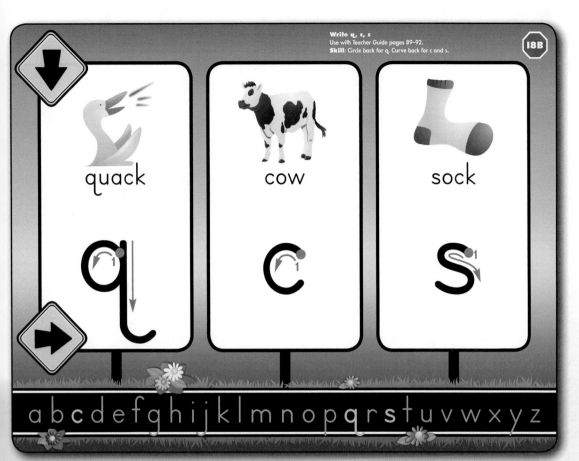

Write q, c, s
Use with Teacher Guide pages 89–92.
Skill: Circle back for q. Curve back for c and s.

18B

quack

cow

sock

a b c d e f g h i j k l m n o p q r s t u v w x y z

Chant
Use this chant to help children remember to use the helper hand when they draw or write.

Helper Hand
Helper hand, helper hand,
Help me write.
Stay flat and hold my paper
As we move from left to right.

Center Time Days 3–5

*Choose multisensory activities for writing practice from the **Center Time** information on pages 18–19 or the activity below.*

Guess the Letter Make a recording that asks children to guess a letter based on a sound clue and a description of its lines. (For **s**: This letter begins the word *surprise*. To write it, curve back, curve forward.) Children can listen, choose the Alphabet Card that matches the stroke description, and then use Wikki Stix to form the letter on the card. As they listen again, children can trace the completed letter with the pointer finger of the writing hand.

Play Time Days 3–5

*Use the **Play Time** information on page 20 and the idea below to introduce purposeful writing into children's dramatic play.*

A New Game Provide a variety of game supplies: beanbags, balls, cones, dice, and pawn-type markers. Challenge small groups of children to make up new games based on the items. Also have writing materials available for making game boards, rules, cards, and signs. Let each group show how to play its game.

Music, Mazes & More CD-ROM

Music for Movement
ABC Rap (Track 2)
Wake Up Fingers (Track 4)
My Two Hands (Track 7)
Circle Song (Track 11)

Optional Practice Pages
You may wish to use some of these practice pages in the writing center.

Mazes: Pages 3, 7, 10–12
Picture/Letter Cards: Pages 13–18
Letters: Pages 59, 73, 75

Fun With Fundamentals

See pages 10–13 for additional information about the development of these essential skills.

Developing Gross-Motor Skills

Blow up balloons and use a permanent marker to write **q**, **c**, or **s** on each one. Play lively music as children toss and bat the balloons. When the music stops, have children freeze and call out a word that begins with the letter on the balloon they are holding.

Developing Fine-Motor Skills

Continue to develop scissor skills. While opening and closing the scissor blades, the fingers and thumb remain curved—there should be no straight fingers. To help with this position, have the child press a small piece of sponge against the palm with the ring and pinky fingers when cutting.

As children progress from cutting stiff materials (such as sandpaper and old greeting cards) to regular paper, remind them to use the helper hand to hold the paper taut within the blades. Draw patterns on paper for children to cut, proceeding from short straight lines, to longer straight lines, to curved lines, to shapes.

Developing Print Awareness

On chart paper, write a new story about Cow and Duck. Let children help by giving story ideas and matching sounds to letters they know. When the story is complete, invite volunteers to measure the spaces between words with a small block, the soft end of a thick paintbrush, or the width of several fingertips.

Developing Letter Recognition

Distribute Letter Magnets. Then sing: "If you have a **c** in your lap, give a clap. If you have a **c** in your lap, don't be shy, give a clap". Repeat for other letters, making up a new motion for each letter.

Developing Sound-Symbol Awareness

From the *Music, Mazes & More* CD-ROM, print Practice Pages 13–18. Cut apart the cards and let children match uppercase and lowercase letters to pictures whose names begin with the matching sounds.

Featured Letters

Objectives
- Recognize the letters **j, g**
- Write curve back lines
- Write the letters **j, g**
- Listen to a story
- Develop oral language and writing skills

Kit Materials
- Group Time Card 19
- *Music, Mazes & More* CD-ROM
- Alphabet Cards **j, g**
- Magnetic Letters and Board
- Touch and Trace Letter Cards **j, g**
- Wikki Stix®

Classroom Materials
- Drawing paper, crayons, glue
- Brown or green pipe cleaners
- Pretend zoo supplies
- Sponges, bowls of water, chalkboard, chalk
- Masking tape
- "Jungle" snack such as fruit slices

Stroke Focus

Curve back.

Letter Focus

1. Pull down.
   Curve back.
2. Dot.

1. Circle back.
   Push up.
   Pull down.
   Curve back.

Teacher Tips

The letters **j** and **g** have "tails" that curve back to the left. Do some practice up front with the curve back line to help children avoid reversing these letters. Using a highlighter, write several curve back lines across children's papers. As you write each, say "curve back." Let children use crayons to write over your highlighted strokes. Help them mark the left edge of the paper and emphasize that "curve back" means curving to the left.

The letter **g** is a mirror-twin for **q**. In this lesson, closely associate **g** with **j** to help with correct directionality. Since children will rarely use **q** in their writing, emphasize **g**'s shape—a "ball" (circle) with a curve directly underneath to catch it. What other lowercase letters begin by circling or curving back? (**o, a, d, s, c**) Use circle back letters to write words like **gas** and **dog**.

Stroke Story

Children act out motions shown in red.

Gorilla lived at the zoo. One day, she was with her cousins outside. They were playing a favorite game—grabbing a rope with the right arm, swinging to grab a rope with the left arm, then jumping down. (Swing right arm, then left, then jump.)

When Gorilla swung high, she noticed something across the yard. It was the zookeeper. Gorilla wondered what the keeper was doing. Maybe today he would bring bananas, or a new toy. Gorilla was very curious.

Gorilla snuck away from her cousins. (Walk like a gorilla, with fists swinging.) She spied something on a log. The zookeeper had left something new. It was liquid, like water, but brightly colored. It looked good to taste.

Gorilla climbed a tree over the tasty-looking thing. She put her arm straight down, but she couldn't reach. (Reach straight down with writing arm.) She climbed down the tree and hid behind it. She slid her arm straight out, but she still couldn't reach. (Reach straight out with writing arm.)

Feeling brave, Gorilla grabbed a branch overhead, swung out, and curved her long arm down. (Curve writing hand down and left in a j shape.) She lifted the smooth glass and drank the cool, colored water. Yum! This must be what the keeper called juice!

94

Learn j, g
Use with Teacher Guide pages 93–96.
Skill: These letters have "tails" that curve back to the left.

19A

abcdefghijklmnopqrstuvwxyz

Group Time Days 1–2

*Gather children together for group time. Use the **Group Time** information on pages 16–17 and the notes below.*

Group Time Card 19A

1. Warm up with a song. Choose one listed at right.
2. Tell the Stroke Story.
3. Trace the arrow beside the gorilla's arm. Say "curve back."
4. Sing "ABC Rap." Point to the target letters in yellow on the Alphabet Road.
5. Sky-write curve back lines in **j** and **g**. For each, say "curve back."

Group Time Card 19B

1. Warm up with a song. Choose one listed at right.
2. Sing "ABC Rap." Point to the letters on the Alphabet Road. Clap when you come to **g** and **j**.

3. Talk about letter shapes. Both letters have a curved tail. If **g** drops its ball (circle), the tail will catch it; if **j** drops its ball (dot), the tail will catch it. Read the word for each letter. Find the letter in the word. Who has these letters in his or her name?
4. Sky-write each letter several times, beginning at the green dot and following the arrows. Say the name of each line aloud.
5. Write a message, such as "Gorilla guzzles grape juice," using shared or interactive writing. Point to letters, words, and spaces.

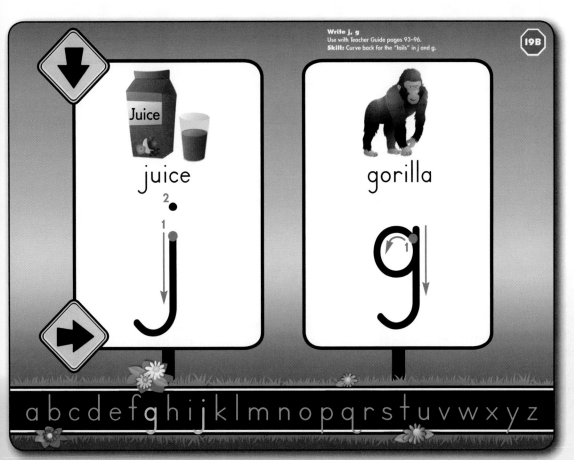

Write j, g
Use with Teacher Guide pages 93–96.
Skill: Curve back for the "tails" in j and g.

19B

juice

gorilla

a b c d e f g h i j k l m n o p q r s t u v w x y z

Chant
Use this chant to remind children how to write in the sky.

Sky-Writing
I draw a paper in the sky.
I hold two fingers way up high.
I draw big lines and letters, too.
I'm sky-writing—so can you!

2 Center Time Days 3–5

*Choose multisensory activities for writing practice from the **Center Time** information on pages 18–19 or the activity below.*

Jungle Letters Show how to crayon a banana tree near the left edge of a sheet of drawing paper; put an arrow pointing left on the tree. Distribute green or brown pipe cleaners and help children use them to fashion **j** and **g** shapes. Show how to glue the letters onto the paper with the curved tails pointing toward the banana tree. Have children crayon a dot for **j** and a jungle scene all around. They may trace the completed letters, saying the names of the lines aloud.

3 Play Time Days 3–5

*Use the **Play Time** information on page 20 and the idea below to introduce purposeful writing into children's dramatic play.*

Zoo Have children make a zoo. They may wish to take on animal roles themselves or use toy animals they find in your classroom. Have nonfiction books about animals and maps or brochures from a local zoo available. Some children may wish to be veterinarians, animal caretakers, or dieticians (who prepare the animals' food). Provide writing materials for making signs with facts about the animals.

Music, Mazes & More CD-ROM

Music for Movement
Sky-Writing (Track 1)
Thumbs Up (Track 5)
Hold Your Crayon (Track 8)
I Pull Down (Track 9)

Optional Practice Pages
You may wish to use some of these practice pages in the writing center.

Mazes: Pages 3, 7, 10–12
Picture/Letter Cards: Pages 13–18
Letters: Pages 63, 66

95

Fun With Fundamentals

See pages 10–13 for additional information about the development of these essential skills.

Developing Fine-Motor Skills

Let children dip sponges in bowls of water and squeeze the writing hand tightly to wring them out. Small pieces of wet sponge may be used to write lines and letters on the chalkboard or on an outdoor wall. Try writing or drawing with chalk, letting children trace over your lines with their wet sponges.

Developing Spatial Awareness

Make a line down the center of the room with masking tape. Talk about which side of the room is to the right of the line and which side is to the left (based on the direction children are facing). Then give a series of commands to go to the right or left. For example, say: "Boys go to the left; girls go to the right," or "Children with lace-up shoes go to the left."

Developing Letter Recognition

Hide Letter Magnets around the room in plain sight. Invite children to go on a jungle hunt to find hidden letters. When children bring letters to you and correctly name them, reward them with a jungle snack such as fruit slices. When all letters are found, arrange them together in alphabetical order.

Developing Sound-Symbol Awareness

Say "gorilla," emphasizing the beginning sound. Then say a series of words, such as *girl, house, dog, gate, baby,* and *gift.* When children hear a word that begins with /**g**/, they should move around like a gorilla. Repeat with other animal motions, such as moving like a fish for words that begin with /**f**/.

Developing Handwriting Skills

Continue to emphasize a correct and comfortable writing grip. Monitor children's hand positions frequently so that awkward grips aren't allowed to become habits. To correct a child's grip, speak directly to his or her fingers. For example, say: "Thumb, you're letting the crayon fall! Hold it up!" Model the three-finger or tripod grip shown on page 13.

Featured Letters

Objectives

- Recognize the letters **b, p, r**
- Write circle forward and curve forward lines
- Write the letters **b, p, r**
- Listen to a story
- Develop oral language and writing skills

Kit Materials

- Group Time Card 20
- *Music, Mazes & More* CD-ROM
- Alphabet Cards **b, p, r**
- Magnetic Letters and Board
- Touch and Trace Letter Cards **b, p, r**
- Wikki Stix®

Classroom Materials

- Cornstarch and water
- Blue food coloring
- Trays or foil pans
- Toy boats
- Materials to create a pirate sea
- Dry beans, peas, rice
- Bowls, plastic tweezers
- Small stickers, circle stencil
- Blank paper, markers
- Yellow construction paper
- Shoebox, tape
- Chart paper

Stroke Focus

Circle forward.

Curve forward.

Letter Focus

I. Pull down.
Push up.
Circle forward.

I. Pull down.
Push up.
Circle forward.

I. Pull down.
Push up.
Curve forward.

Teacher Tips

Each letter in this lesson requires the crayon to retrace the vertical line before curving forward in a circle (**b** and **p**) or arc (**r**). Combining these motions smoothly will be a challenge for many preschoolers.

Let children steer toy boats to practice the retracing or push up motion. Make a vertical line on the floor with tape and ask children to move the boat from top to bottom, turn, and sail back up on the same line.

Because children have been writing circle back letters (such as **o, a, d, g**), the circle forward motion may seem new. Practice clockwise circles that begin at 9:00 by sky-writing or writing in trays of sand or salt. Use Wikki Stix to make a circle and a vertical line and demonstrate how to change **b** to **p** by moving the vertical line up and down. Associating **b** with other circle forward and curve forward letters will help children avoid confusing it with **d**. Emphasize that **b** begins at the top.

Stroke Story

Children act out motions shown in red.

When Parrot was on his ship, he was called Pirate Red Beard. He stood at the helm, steering the wheel and looking out for trouble.

When Parrot stood beside the wheel, it looked like **b** in **bird**. (Fist right hand and hold it against the palm of upright left hand to make b shape.) When Parrot curled his thick feet around the wheel to hang upside down, it looked like **p** in **pirate**. (Fist right hand and hold it against fingers of upright left hand to make p shape.) And when Parrot stood tall on the deck of his ship, with his beak curving forward, he looked like **r** in **red**. (Hold left hand upright and curve fingers to make r shape.)

One day Parrot captured a chest of gold coins and jeweled rings from enemy pirates. The enemies attacked Parrot's ship, looking for their treasure. But Pirate Red Beard was brave. He flew at the intruders, making gold coins spin in the air. (Circle pointer finger of writing hand in clockwise circles in the air.) He chased the enemies away, then turned the ship's wheel hard to make his escape. (Turn ship's wheel to right.)

Pirate Red Beard rang the ship's bell. He ruled the seas!

Learn b, p, r
Use with Teacher Guide pages 97–100.
Skill: Each of these letters has a forward circle or forward curve.
20A

b p r

a b c d e f g h i j k l m n o p q r s t u v w x y z

Group Time Days 1–2

*Gather children together for group time. Use the **Group Time** information on pages 16–17 and the notes below.*

Group Time Card 20A

1. Warm up with a song. Choose one listed at right.
2. Tell the Stroke Story.
3. Trace the arrow near the wheel; make it a complete circle. Say "circle forward." Trace the arrow in a partial circle. Say "curve forward."
4. Sing "ABC Rap." Point to the target letters in yellow on the Alphabet Road.
5. Sky-write circle forward lines in **b** and **p**. For each, say "circle forward." Sky-write the curve forward line in **r**. Say "curve forward."

Group Time Card 20B

1. Warm up with a song. Choose one listed at right.

2. Sing "ABC Rap." Point to the letters on the Alphabet Road. Clap when you come to **b, p**, and **r**.
3. Talk about letter shapes. Each letter has a stick (pull down line) with a ball (circle) or curve sticking out. Who has these letters in his or her name? Find the letters in the room. Read the word for each letter. Find the letter in the word.
4. Sky-write each letter several times, beginning at the green dot and following the arrows. Say the name of each line aloud.
5. Write a message, such as "Parrot rings the pirate bell," using shared or interactive writing. Read the message together, pointing to letters, words, and spaces.

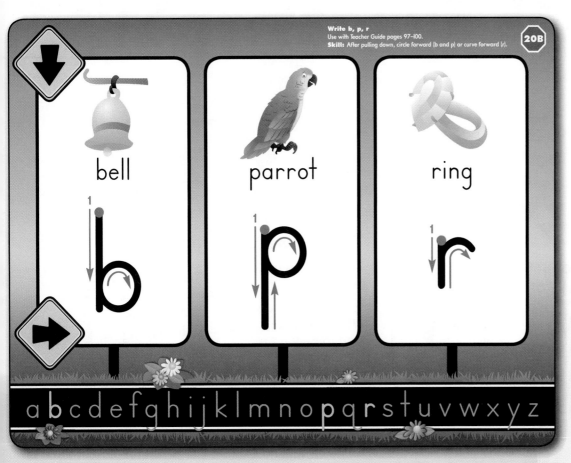

Write b, p, r
Use with Teacher Guide pages 97–100.
Skills: After pulling down, circle forward (b and p) or curve forward (r).

20B

bell

parrot

ring

a b c d e f g h i j k l m n o p q r s t u v w x y z

Chant
Use this chant with uppercase or lowercase alphabet cards to help children with letter recognition.

I Spy a Letter
I spy a letter.
Can you see?
It might be A.
It could be Z.
Here's a clue:
It looks like _____.
Here's a clue:
It sounds like _____.
Can you guess it?
It's a letter you've met.
It's part of
The alphabet!

Music, Mazes & More CD-ROM

Music for Movement
ABC Rap (Track 2)
Top to Bottom (Track 3)
I Pull Down (Track 9)
Circle Song (Track 11)

Optional Practice Pages
You may wish to use some of these practice pages in the writing center.

Mazes: Pages 1–3, 5–7, 10–12
Picture/Letter Cards: Pages 13–18
Letters: Pages 58, 72, 74

 Center Time Days 3–5

*Choose multisensory activities for writing practice from the **Center Time** information on pages 18–19 or the activity below.*

Ship Shapes Mix cornstarch and water to make "goop." Use food coloring to color the goop blue and spread a thick layer in several trays or large foil pans. Provide small toy boats and let each child steer a boat in the goop sea in the shape of the letters **b, p,** and **r**. Display Alphabet Cards to show the correct stroke sequence for each letter. Remind children that the boats should turn around and sail back the other direction to "push up" at the end of each pull down line.

3 Play Time Days 3–5

*Use the **Play Time** information on page 20 and the idea below to introduce purposeful writing into children's dramatic play.*

Pirates Spread a large laminated map of the world on the floor. Let children sail toy boats or paper boats on the seven seas. Provide crayons, scissors, and tape so children can name their ships and outfit them with flags and treasure chests.

Fun With Fundamentals

See pages 10–13 for additional information about the development of these essential skills.

Developing Gross-Motor Skills

Let children pretend to be parrots or other birds as you give directions for moving and flying around. For example, say: "Flap your left wing," "Fly in a forward circle," or "Stand on your right foot."

Developing Fine-Motor Skills

In a large bowl, mix dry <u>b</u>eans, <u>p</u>eas, and <u>r</u>ice. Provide plastic tweezers and show how to hold and squeeze them with the thumb and pointer finger of the writing hand to pick up the small items and sort them into three smaller bowls labeled "**b**," "**p**," and "**r**." This motion builds finger strength and control. Try moving the items to blank construction paper to make a collage picture. (Picking up the items with fingers instead of tweezers is a good exercise, too.)

Developing Spatial Awareness

Let children put small stickers on paper in a circle shape. (It may help to provide a circle stencil made of cardstock to guide sticker placement.) Provide markers and show how to draw a green circle around the sticker placed at about the 9:00 position. Beginning at that sticker, children can use a marker to connect the stickers with a circle forward line.

Developing Letter Recognition

Cut circles from yellow construction paper to be "gold coins." Write a lowercase letter on each coin and place them in a shoebox "treasure chest." Let children pick coins from the box and name the letters. Then stick the coins to a wall or chalkboard with loops of tape. Let children arrange them to spell names and words.

Developing Sound-Symbol Awareness

On chart paper, write "I sailed on a ship and brought…" Use the coins from the previous activity. When each child draws a coin, ask him or her to name something that begins with the letter. Add the word to the chart paper list. For example, "I sailed on a ship and brought bunnies" (for **b**).

Featured Letters

n m h

Objectives
- Recognize the letters **n, m, h**
- Write forward curves
- Write the letters **n, m, h**
- Listen to a story
- Develop oral language and writing skills

Kit Materials
- Group Time Card 21
- *Music, Mazes & More* CD-ROM
- Alphabet Cards **n, m, h**
- Magnetic Letters and Board
- Touch and Trace Letter Cards **n, m, h**
- Wikki Stix®

Classroom Materials
- Blank paper, crayons
- Glitter glue
- Materials for an Invention Center
- Scented markers
- Alphabet picture books
- Muffin pan, tape
- Apron with large pockets or a box

Stroke Focus

Curve forward.

Letter Focus

1. Pull down.
   Push up.
   Curve forward.

1. Pull down.
   Push up.
   Curve forward.
   Push up.
   Curve forward.

1. Pull down.
   Push up.
   Curve forward.

Teacher Tips

The letters in this lesson require writers to push up, or retrace the vertical line, before curving forward. Help children practice the pull down/push up/curve forward motion slowly and carefully to avoid gaps and double lines. Let them paint or write a pattern of continuous curve forward "humps" on large sheets of paper or across the chalkboard.

The letter **m** has an additional retrace at the center—the right side of the first "hump" is retraced before beginning the second. Remind children that **m**'s hills should be close together so that a child could jump from one to the other without falling down in between. It may help to form a large **m** with masking tape on the floor so that children can walk along its shape.

Praise children for beginning each letter at the top left and for their attempts to write curve forward lines. Mastery of the letter shapes will come with practice over the years to come.

Stroke Story

Children act out motions shown in red.

Moose was the biggest, friendliest animal in the forest. The small animals loved to play with him. Bird rode on his back. Chipmunk ran around his tall legs.

Mouse scrambled up onto Moose's antlers. She climbed each hump and slid down the other side—up and curve, up and curve, up and curve. (Volunteers trace antler curves on Group Time card; others use pointer finger of writing hand to sky-write a row of curve forward lines.)

Moose wanted to play and climb and curve, too. Why should the little animals have all the fun? He had an idea. He cut down a tree and used its wood to build a car. He built a ramp, too. He worked hard, swinging his hammer as he sang a little song: up and curve, up and curve, up and curve. (Swing hammer to the right with writing arm.)

Finally, the toys were ready. Riding in the car, Moose went up the ramp and curved fast down the other side. (Bend helper hand in ramp shape; use pointer finger of writing hand to trace path up and over.) "Whee," Moose called to his little friends. "Come and take a ride!"

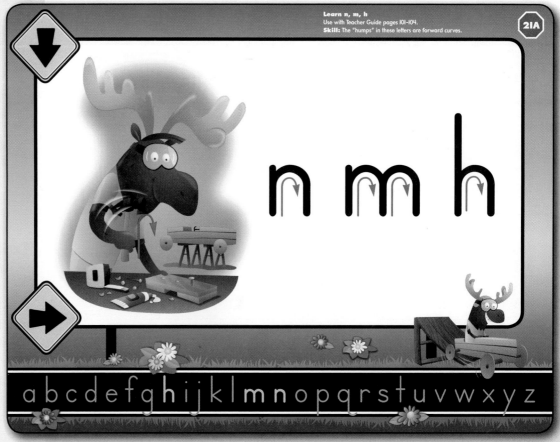

Learn n, m, h
Use with Teacher Guide pages 101–104.
Skill: The "humps" in these letters are forward curves.

21A

a b c d e f g h i j k l m n o p q r s t u v w x y z

Group Time Days 1–2

*Gather children together for group time. Use the **Group Time** information on pages 16–17 and the notes below.*

Group Time Card 21A

1. Warm up with a song. Choose one listed at right.
2. Tell the Stroke Story.
3. Trace the arrow near the hammer. Say "curve forward."
4. Sing "ABC Rap." Point to the target letters in yellow on the Alphabet Road.
5. Sky-write curve forward lines in **n, m,** and **h.** For each, say "curve forward."

Group Time Card 21B

1. Warm up with a song. Choose one listed at right.
2. Sing "ABC Rap." Point to the letters on the Alphabet Road. Clap when you come to **h, m,** and **n.**

3. Talk about letter shapes. They all have pull down lines and humps, or curves; **n** and **h** have one hump; **m** has two. The letter **n** can be seen inside **m.** Who has these letters in his or her name? Read the word for each letter. Find the letter in the word.
4. Sky-write each letter several times, beginning at the green dot and following the arrows. Say the name of each line aloud.
5. Write a message, such as "Moose hammers a nail," using shared or interactive writing. Read the message together, pointing to letters, words, and spaces.

102

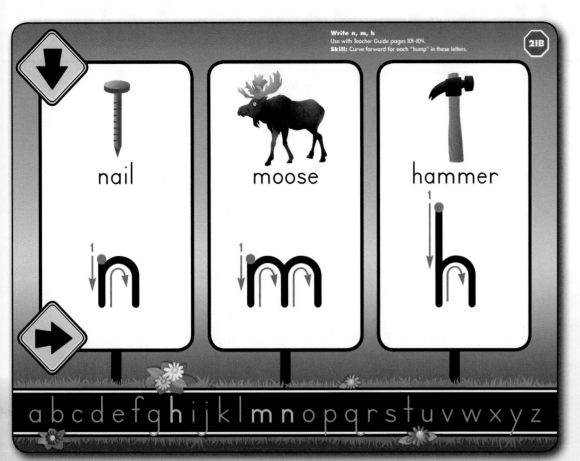

Write n, m, h
Use with Teacher Guide pages 101-104.
Skill: Curve forward for each "hump" in these letters.

21B

nail

moose

hammer

n

m

h

a b c d e f g h i j k l m n o p q r s t u v w x y z

Chant

Use this chant to help children remember to use the helper hand when they draw or write.

Helper Hand

Helper hand, helper hand,
Help me write.
Stay flat and hold my paper
As we move from left to right.

---

2 Center Time Days 3–5

Choose multisensory activities for writing practice from the **Center Time** *information on pages 18–19 or the activity below.*

Touch and Trace Supply Touch and Trace Letter Cards **Nn, Mm,** and **Hh**. Show how to trace each letter with the pointer finger of the writing hand as the helper hand secures the card. Emphasize the correct starting point and stroke sequence. As they trace, children should say the name of each line aloud. They can then use paper and crayons to make letter rubbings. Show how to squeeze a thick bead of glitter glue inside each letter rubbing. When the glue dries, children can trace the dimensional letters.

3 Play Time Days 3–5

Use the **Play Time** *information on page 20 and the idea below to introduce purposeful writing into children's dramatic play.*

Inventors, Inc. Provide a box of materials for inventing—wood and foam pieces, string, clothespins and clamps, paperclips, cardboard, cloth, etc. When a child completes an invention, ask him or her to write a label for it as well as simple directions for its use. Let children explain their inventions to the class.

Music, Mazes & More CD-ROM

Music for Movement
ABC Rap (Track 2)
Thumbkin (Track 6)
Hold Your Crayon (Track 8)
I Pull Down (Track 9)

Optional Practice Pages
You may wish to use some of these practice pages in the writing center.

Mazes: Pages 1, 2, 5, 6, 9, 10, 12
Picture/Letter Cards: Pages 13–18
Letters: Pages 64, 69, 70.

Fun With Fundamentals

See pages 10–13 for additional information about the development of these essential skills.

Developing Fine-Motor Skills

Completing mazes helps children build eye control and coordination, hand control, and motor planning. Print copies of the mazes on Practice Pages 1–12 from the *Music, Mazes & More* CD-ROM. Let children complete them with fun writing tools such as scented markers. Encourage children to design and complete their own mazes, too.

Developing Print Awareness

Collect a variety of alphabet picture books from your classroom or local library so that each child has one. Say the alphabet slowly together as children page through their books, touching and tracing letters and calling out pictured items that begin with each letter.

Developing Letter Recognition

Print Practice Pages 17–18 from the *Music, Mazes & More* CD-ROM for each child. Cut apart the lowercase letters and give 12 familiar letters to each child. Tape the same 12 letters to a muffin pan to label the 12 cups. Then have children sort their letters into the matching muffin cups.

Developing Sound-Symbol Awareness

Become a letter-sound robot for children to use. Wear an apron with a large pocket or hold a box on your lap. When children drop in a Letter Magnet, come to life and use a robot voice to say words that begin with the letter's sound. Let children try being the robot, too.

Developing Handwriting Skills

Continue to remind children to let the helper hand, or non-writing hand, assist them when they write. The helper hand should be visible on the tabletop, securing the paper and shifting it as needed. Encourage children to use the helper hand to hold puzzle frames while the dominant hand moves pieces, to grip jacket hems when zipping up, and to steady paper within scissor blades.

Featured Letters

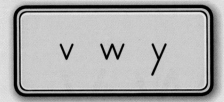

Objectives
- Recognize the letters **v, w, y**
- Write slant right lines
- Write the letters **v, w, y**
- Listen to a story
- Develop oral language and writing skills

Kit Materials
- Group Time Card 22
- *Music, Mazes & More* CD-ROM
- Alphabet Cards **v, w, y**
- Magnetic Letters and Board
- Touch and Trace Letter Cards **v, w, y**
- Wikki Stix®

Classroom Materials
- Overhead projector, yardstick or long pointer
- Materials to set up Story Street
- Small magnets
- Small metal objects such as paper clips
- Dusting cloths
- Fairy tale picture books
- Four brooms or mops

Stroke Focus

Slant right.

Letter Focus

I. Slant right.
   Slant up.

I. Slant right.
   Slant up.
   Slant right.
   Slant up.

I. Slant right.
2. Slant left.

Teacher Tips

If it has been some time since children worked with uppercase **V, W,** and **Y,** this lesson provides a good opportunity for additional practice with slant lines. Look at an alphabet chart together (like the one on Group Time Card 25) and recognize that the lowercase letters are identical or similar to the familiar uppercase letters.

Slant strokes present motor and perceptual challenges for young writers. Preschoolers may be unsure where to start slant strokes, or where to aim. They may enjoy dot-to-dot exercises for completing the down-and-up motions for **v** and **w.** Make sure to model lifting the crayon to begin **y**'s second stroke at the top. Although the upper part of **y** resembles **v,** the stroke sequence is different.

Stroke Story

Children act out motions shown in red.

Early in the morning, Wolf jumped out of his bed, ready to start the day. He stretched his arms up high. (Stretch.) With his legs together, he stretched down to touch his toes. (Stretch.) With his legs stretched wide, he slanted his arm down to touch his left foot. (Touch left foot with writing hand.) He slanted his arm down to touch his right foot. (Touch right foot with writing hand.)

After breakfast, it was time to clean the house. He pushed a button to make the vacuum cleaner slant, and he started to clean the floors. (Slant writing arm down to the right and bend at the elbow several times, pretending to vacuum the floor.) He slanted his yellow duster down to clean the legs of a chair. (Slant writing arm down and right to dust.) He reached under a table to pick up some crayons that had dropped. (Slant writing arm down and right to pick up several crayons.)

When the house was clean, Wolf did a little dance. He boogied while he slanted his paw up and down. (Point up to the right then down to the right with pointer finger of writing hand.)

Now what else did Wolf have to do today? Oh, yes, he would pay a visit to those little pigs!

Learn v, w, y
Use with Teacher Guide pages 105–108.
Skill: These letters have slant right lines.
22A

v w y

a b c d e f g h i j k l m n o p q r s t u v w x y z

Group Time Days 1–2

*Gather children together for group time. Use the **Group Time** information on pages 16–17 and the notes below.*

Group Time Card 22A

1. Warm up with a song. Choose one listed at right.
2. Tell the Stroke Story.
3. Trace the arrow near the vacuum. Say "slant right."
4. Sing "ABC Rap." Point to the target letters in yellow on the Alphabet Road.
5. Sky-write the slant right lines in **v**, **w**, and **y** and say "slant right."

Group Time Card 22B

1. Warm up with a song. Choose one listed at right.
2. Sing "ABC Rap." Point to the letters on the Alphabet Road. Clap when you come to **v**, **w**, and **y**.

3. Talk about letter shapes. The letters **v** and **w** look like upside-down mountains; **y** is like **v** with a long handle at the bottom. Who has these letters in his or her name? Can these letters be found in the classroom? Read the word for each letter. Find the letter in the word.
4. Sky-write each letter several times, beginning at the green dot and following the arrows. Say the name of each line aloud.
5. Write a message, such as "Wolf is a very wild dancer," using shared or interactive writing. Read the message together, pointing to letters, words, and spaces.

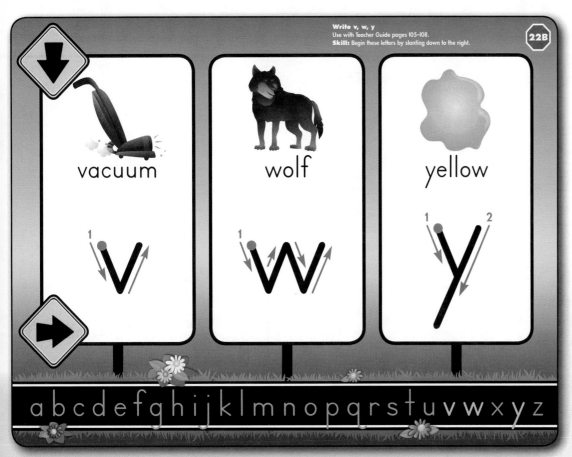

Write v, w, y
Use with Teacher Guide pages 105–108.
Skill: Begin these letters by slanting down to the right.

22B

vacuum

wolf

yellow

a b c d e f g h i j k l m n o p q r s t u v w x y z

Chant
Use this chant with uppercase or lowercase alphabet cards to help children with letter recognition.

I Spy a Letter
I spy a letter.
Can you see?
It might be A.
It could be Z.
Here's a clue:
It looks like _____.
Here's a clue:
It sounds like _____.
Can you guess it?
It's a letter you've met.
It's part of
The alphabet!

Music, Mazes & More CD-ROM

Music for Movement
Sky-Writing (Track 1)
ABC Rap (Track 2)
Thumbs Up (Track 5)
Slant Dance (Track 12)

Optional Practice Pages
You may wish to use some of these practice pages in the writing center.

Mazes: Pages 4, 8
Picture/Letter Cards: Pages 13–18
Letters: Pages 78, 79, 81

2 Center Time Days 3–5

*Choose multisensory activities for writing practice from the **Center Time** information on pages 18–19 or the activity below.*

Light Letters Let children use Wikki Stix to form **v, w**, and **y** on an overhead projector. Project the images on a wall or screen. Some children can trace the Wikki Stix letters with their fingers and say the name of each line as others watch the projected image. Others may use a yardstick or long pointer to trace the projected letters, again saying the name of each line aloud.

3 Play Time Days 3–5

*Use the **Play Time** information on page 20 and the idea below to introduce purposeful writing into children's dramatic play.*

Story Street Let individuals or small groups of children set up house as fairy tale characters such as the big bad wolf, the three pigs, and Cinderella. Encourage children to establish a mailbox for each character's house. Provide fairy tale picture books as references. Provide writing materials for making street signs, house numbers, mail to deliver, and other story props, such as invitations from the king.

Fun With Fundamentals

See pages 10–13 for additional information about the development of these essential skills.

Developing Fine-Motor Skills

To encourage refinement of elbow movements, try this idea. Print and laminate several mazes from the *Music, Mazes & More* CD-ROM. Have a child hold a maze with the helper hand and hold a small magnet underneath the maze with the writing hand. Put a small metal object such as a paper clip on top and have the child guide it through the maze by moving the magnet.

Developing Spatial Awareness

Distribute dusting cloths for cleaning the classroom. Then give spatial commands as children dust. For example, say "Slant down to the right to dust the toys on the bottom shelf," or "Slant up to the right to dust the window sill."

Developing Print Awareness

Set out a collection of fairy tale picture books and examine their titles. Ask children to point out letters they know, such as **w** in "Snow White," and match them to letters they see in the classroom or letters on Group Time Card 25B.

Developing Letter Recognition

Use four brooms or mops on the floor of a large, open area to form the shapes of **v, w,** and **y**. Challenge children to identify the letters and to find **v** within **w** and **y**. A large pointer may be used to trace the letters. Can the four tools be used to make other letters?

Developing Handwriting Skills

Left-Handed Writers: Recognize the needs of children who have clearly demonstrated a preference for the left hand. Demonstrate a good grip, shown on page 13, and suggest holding the writing tool slightly farther back so they can see their writing. The helper hand should adjust the position of the paper to avoid a "hooked" grip.

Featured Letters

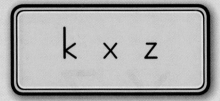

Objectives
- Recognize the letters **k, x, z**
- Write slant left lines
- Write the letters **k, x, z**
- Listen to a story
- Develop oral language and writing skills

Kit Materials
- Group Time Card 23
- *Music, Mazes & More* CD-ROM
- Alphabet Cards **k, x, z**
- Magnetic Letters and Board
- Touch and Trace Letter Cards **k, x, z**
- Wikki Stix®

Classroom Materials
- Plain envelopes
- Paper grocery bags, masking tape, green markers
- Materials to set up a classroom post office
- Sand, rice
- Paper, envelopes, stickers
- 26 envelopes
- Old newspapers or magazines
- Child-sized scissors
- 3–8 shoeboxes

Stroke Focus

Slant left.

Letter Focus

1. Pull down.
2. Slant left.
   Slant right.

1. Slant right.
2. Slant left.

1. Slide.
   Slant left.
   Slide.

Teacher Tips

Take time to review left and right as children write the letters in this lesson. Slant lines are named for the direction in which they slant. So, slant left lines begin at right and slant down toward the left. They might also be called "slant back" lines because they move toward the left, breaking the rule that written lines progress from left to right.

Writing slant lines can be difficult for young writers, and the left/right distinction may add another level of confusion. Provide help by marking a green dot where slant lines should begin and a red dot where they should end. Practice sky-writing each letter slowly, naming its lines aloud.

As children spend more time writing on their own, check daily to make sure they are holding the writing tool correctly (as shown on page 13) and beginning each letter at the correct starting point. Developing these habits now will give children a strong foundation for writing success in the years to come.

Stroke Story

Children act out motions shown in red. Give each child a plain envelope to use during the story.

As the envelopes and boxes came down the ramp, Koala loaded them into her delivery bag. Koala would deliver the letters and packages to people on her route. She knew that the mail had taken a long journey before it got to her bag.

Do you know what happens when you mail a letter? First, you write to your friend. You put the letter in an envelope and write the address. *(Write pretend letter, put in envelope, and address.)* Then you open the big blue mailbox *(open door with helper hand)* and slant your letter down inside. *(With writing hand, slant envelope left into mailbox.)*

After the letter is picked up, it goes to the post office and gets lifted and turned and sorted by machines. *(Slant envelope left through machines.)* Then it travels by truck *(bump envelope along)* or by airplane *(soar envelope overhead)* to the town where your friend lives. At another post office, it gets sorted and put in the mail carrier's bag. *(Slant envelope left into bag.)* Finally, it is delivered to your friend's house.

Koala's bag is loaded. She is ready to deliver the mail. Maybe she will come to your house!

Learn k, x, z
Use with Teacher Guide pages 109–112.
Skill: Each of these letters contains a slant left line.

23A

k x z

a b c d e f g h i j k l m n o p q r s t u v w x y z

Group Time Days 1–2

*Gather children together for group time. Use the **Group Time** information on pages 16–17 and the notes below.*

Group Time Card 23A

1. Warm up with a song. Choose one listed at right.
2. Tell the Stroke Story.
3. Trace the arrow beside the ramp. Say "slant left."
4. Sing "ABC Rap." Point to the target letters in yellow on the Alphabet Road.
5. Sky-write slant left lines in **k, x,** and **z**. For each, say "slant left."

Group Time Card 23B

1. Warm up with a song. Choose one listed at right.
2. Sing "ABC Rap." Point to the letters on the Alphabet Road. Clap when you come to **k, x,** and **z.**

3. Talk about letter shapes. The letters **x** and **z** are shaped just like their uppercase parents; **k** is tall like its parent, but its kicking arm and leg (slant lines) are lower to the ground. Read the word for each letter. Find the letter in the word. Who has these letters in his or her name?
4. Sky-write each letter several times, beginning at the green dot and following the arrows. Say the name of each line aloud.
5. Write a message, such as "Koala is not lazy. She brings boxes every day," using shared or interactive writing. Point to letters, words, and spaces.

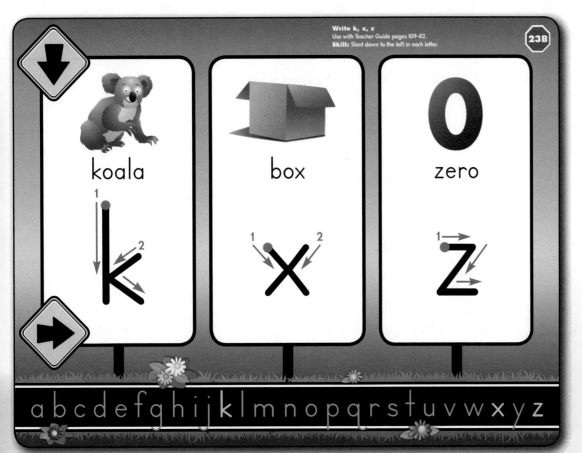

Write k, x, z
Use with Teacher Guide pages 109–112.
Skill: Slant down to the left in each letter.

23B

koala

box

0 zero

k   x   z

a b c d e f g h i j **k** l m n o p q r s t u v w **x y z**

Chant
Use this chant to remind children how to write in the sky.

Sky-Writing
I draw a paper in the sky.
I hold two fingers way up high.
I draw big lines and letters, too.
I'm sky-writing—so can you!

2 Center Time Days 3–5

*Choose multisensory activities for writing practice from the **Center Time** information on pages 18–19 or the activity below.*

Alphabet Packages Provide paper grocery bags and help children cut down one side and along the bottom so the brown paper lies flat. Then show how to form **k, x,** and **z** on the paper with strips of masking tape. You may wish to hold the tape roll while children cut their pieces. Remind children to slant their tape pieces to the left in each letter. They can use markers to add a green starting dot and directional arrows to each letter. The completed letters may be traced as children say the names of the lines aloud.

3 Play Time Days 3–5

*Use the **Play Time** information on page 20 and the idea below to introduce purposeful writing into children's dramatic play.*

Post Office Establish a working post office in your classroom. A manila envelope, shoebox, or cubby can serve as a mailbox for each child. A large cardboard box might be the central mailbox for dropping off mail to be sent. Let children take turns creating mail, processing it in a post office area, and delivering. If possible, provide a delivery bag and a toy vehicle "mail truck." Writing supplies could include paper and envelopes, boxes, sticker "stamps," labels, and rubber stamps for postmarking mail.

Music, Mazes & More CD-ROM

Music for Movement
Sky-Writing (Track 1)
Wake Up Fingers (Track 4)
My Two Hands (Track 7)
Slant Dance (Track 12)

Optional Practice Pages
You may wish to use some of these practice pages in the writing center.

Mazes: Pages 1, 2, 4, 5, 8, 9
Picture/Letter Cards: Pages 13–18
Letters: Pages 67, 80, 82

111

Fun With Fundamentals

See pages 10–13 for additional information about the development of these essential skills.

Developing
Gross-Motor Skills

Challenge children to make **k, x,** and **z** with their bodies. They might hold an arm and leg out at a slant for **k,** extend all arms and legs for **x,** and kneel down on the floor for **z,** slanting the torso back toward the joined legs and feet and extending both arms straight out to form the top slide line.

Developing
Fine-Motor Skills

To help develop the arches of the hands, help the child cup the palm to form a deep hollow at the base of the middle finger and hold the hand in an upturned position. Load the palm with small amounts of sand or rice. Encourage the child to make the hollow deeper so you can add more.

Developing
Spatial Awareness

Let children write letters to family members. Have them seal each completed letter in an envelope, then give spatial directions for marking it. Tell children to put a sticker in the top right corner, to write their name in the top left corner, to draw a picture in the bottom left corner, and to write **xo** to mean "kisses and hugs" in the bottom right corner. Help them write the recipient's name in the center.

Developing
Print Awareness

On a wall or bulletin board, attach 26 open envelopes with the flaps facing out. Write a lowercase letter on each envelope. Then have children look through old newspapers and magazines, cut out examples of each letter, and put them in the matching envelopes. Afterward, choose several envelopes and look at the contents together, examining the letter shapes and commenting on differences in font types.

Developing
Letter Recognition

Set up a row of 3–8 shoebox "mailboxes" with a slit cut in the top of each. Write a lowercase letter on each mailbox. Then copy Practice Pages 15–18 for each child and cut apart the letters. Have children put letters into the matching mailboxes.

Featured Numerals

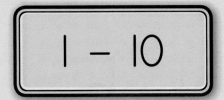

1 – 10

Objectives
- Recognize numerals **1–10**
- Write numerals **1–10**
- Develop oral language and writing skills

Kit Materials
- Group Time Card 24
- *Music, Mazes & More* CD-ROM
- Wikki Stix®
- Blank Story Journal

Classroom Materials
- Plastic counters or chips
- Shaving cream, paper towels
- Shallow lids, play dough, birthday candles
- Construction paper cones and circles
- Glue sticks, crayons
- Giant dice made from foam cubes or cardboard boxes
- Chalkboard and chalk or chart paper and marker
- Supplies to play "office"
- Butcher paper, masking tape, beanbags
- Child-sized scissors, paper
- Stapler, blank paper, crayons
- Laundry baskets or other containers labeled with numerals, toys

1. Pull down.

1. Curve forward.
   Slide right.

1. Curve forward.
   Curve forward.

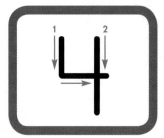

1. Pull down.
   Slide.
2. Pull down.

1. Pull down.
   Circle forward.
2. Slide.

1. Curve down.
   Curve up.

1. Slide.
   Slant left.

1. Curve back.
   Curve forward.

1. Circle back.
   Pull down.

1. Pull down.
2. Curve down.
   Curve up.

Teacher Tips

Let children's interest dictate when writing numerals is introduced. It may be before, during, or after children learn to write uppercase letters. Children will show the most interest in writing numerals that have personal meaning to them, such as the numeral(s) that represent their age, birthdate, and house or apartment number.

Because the ten numerals are written with a variety of lines, it is not practical to teach them according to common strokes. However, you may wish to point out that **1, 4,** and **5** begin with pull down lines, that **7** contains a slant line, and that **2, 3, 6, 8, 9,** and **0** are all formed with curved lines.

When children are encouraged to include writing numerals in their dramatic play, their beginning math skills are greatly enhanced. Don't forget to provide calculators, cash registers, pretend money, numeral magnets, and similar materials when children play. See the Play Time activity in this lesson for suggestions.

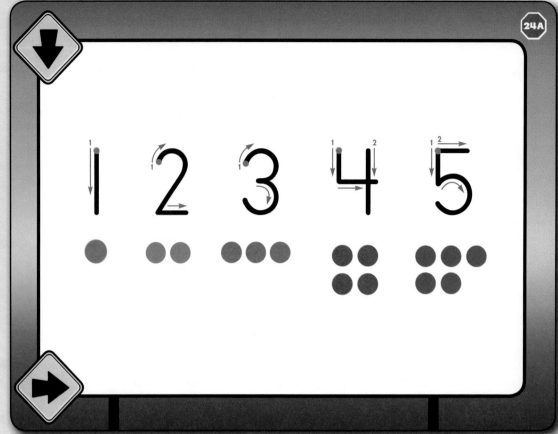

1. Group Time Days 1–2

Gather children together for group time. Use the Group Time information on pages 16–17 and the notes below.

Group Time Cards 24A–24B

1. Warm up with a song. Choose one listed at right.
2. Count each group of dots, then say the name of the corresponding numeral.
3. Sky-write each numeral together, saying the names of its lines aloud.
4. Lay the Group Time Card flat on the floor. Provide Wikki Stix and small objects, such as plastic counters or chips. Let children form each numeral on the card with Wikki Stix and place the objects over the corresponding dots.
5. Show children how to trace the Wikki Stix numerals with the pointer finger of the writing hand, saying the name of each line aloud.

2. Center Time Days 3–5

Choose multisensory activities for writing practice from the Center Time information on pages 18–19 or the activities below.

Count and Clean Dispense shaving cream onto a tabletop. Let children spread out the cream with their fingers. Show either a group of objects or hold up a certain number of fingers. Challenge children to write the corresponding numeral in the shaving cream with the pointer finger of the writing hand. Provide paper towels for cleaning the table.

Candle Counting Set out shallow plastic lids, such as lids from margarine tubs or coffee cans. Invite each child to fill a lid with play dough to make a "birthday cake." Provide birthday candles to press in around the perimeter of the cake. Then ask the child to form the corresponding numeral from play dough and press it into the center of the cake.

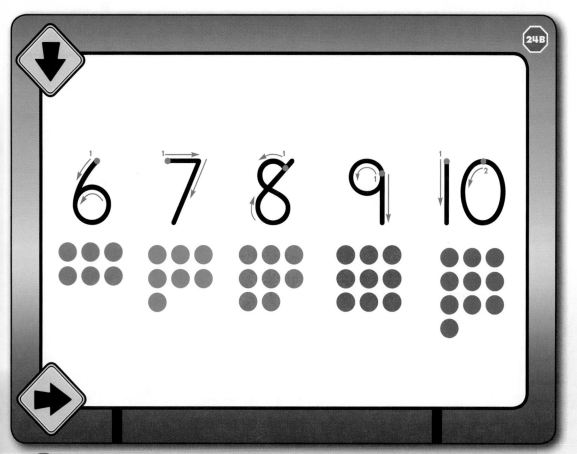

Chant

Use this chant to help children remember how to hold their crayon when they draw or write.

Hold Your Crayon

Crayon, crayon,
Do you want to write?
Jump in my fingers.
I won't hold you tight.

Lean on tall friend,
Pointer on top,
Rest on my thumb,
I won't let you drop.

Ring and pinky
Tuck in beside.
They touch the paper
As we take a ride.

 Center Time Days 3–5

How Many Scoops? Cut construction paper to make, for each child, a brown triangle "cone" and nine different-colored circles. Let children use glue sticks to assemble giant nine-scoop ice cream cones. Ask them to write numerals from **1** to **10** on the shapes, starting with **1** on the cone. Guide children's writing by placing a green starting dot for the numeral to be written on each circle. Together, say the names of the lines in each numeral as children write.

Roll and Write Make two giant dice from foam cubes or cardboard boxes. On the chalkboard or on sheets of chart paper displayed on the wall, write numerals **1–12**. On each child's turn, allow him or her to roll the dice. Count the dots together. Then have the child trace over the matching numeral with chalk, a thick marker, or a finger. As the child traces the numeral, name its lines together.

Play Time Days 3–5

*Use the **Play Time** information on page 20 and the idea below to introduce purposeful writing into children's dramatic play.*

Office Let each child establish a desk space for playing office. Provide small notebooks, calculators, rulers, old checkbooks, toy phones, invoice and receipt pads, old calendars, junk mail, and other office supplies. As they play, encourage children to write numerals to record important information such as phone numbers, dates, expenditures, and amounts owed.

Music, Mazes & More CD-ROM

Music for Movement

Sky-Writing (Track 1)
Top to Bottom (Track 3)
Thumbkin (Track 6)
Hold Your Crayon (Track 8)

Optional Practice Pages

You may wish to use some of these practice pages in the writing center.

Numerals: Pages 83–92

Fun With Fundamentals

See pages 10–13 for additional information about the development of these essential skills.

Developing Gross-Motor Skills

Make a game board on a large sheet of butcher paper. Divide the paper into ten squares and write a numeral in each one. Use masking tape to make a line on the floor. Have children stand behind the line and toss beanbags onto the game board, naming each numeral they hit.

Developing Fine-Motor Skills

Have children use scissors to snip the corners off a sheet of paper. Ask them to count each corner as they cut it. Each cut creates two more corners to count and snip. Continue until the paper is small. Remind children to keep the thumb up as they use scissors. Don't allow it to fall to the side like a "lazy lion."

Developing Print Awareness

Fold and staple paper to make a booklet for each child that has at least one page for each member of the class. Write children's names in the booklet or let children write their classmates' names, one per page. Allow time for children to circulate and write numerals that tell important things about themselves in each other's books, including ages, birthdates, and telephone numbers.

Developing Numeral Recognition

Set up laundry baskets or other containers. On each, tape a sign with a large numeral. Ask children to collect items, such as toys, from the classroom and put the correct number of items in each basket. Mix up the baskets and ask children to put them in numerical order.

Developing Handwriting Skills

As children look at Group Time Card 24, invite them to make observations about numeral shapes. They may point out that **5** and **7** both wear slide line "hats," that **1** is the same as lowercase **l**, or that **10** is two numerals put together. Discuss the fact that **6** has a circle-like shape at the bottom and **9** has a circle at the top. However, arrange for children to practice **6** and **9** on different days so the numerals won't be confused.

Use this informal assessment to evaluate children's readiness for kindergarten handwriting instruction. If possible, assess children's skills through observation of classroom activities over several days or weeks. This is better than testing children on a specific day. Give children ample opportunities to show their skills through verbal responses, nonverbal responses, and physical movement. For example, let children show they recognize letters by naming them or pointing to them on a chart. Let children show they can write letters by sky-writing them in the air. Remember that children will continue to develop all the skills shown here as they grow as writers in the years to come.

Gross-Motor Skills

- Participates in action song motions, following the teacher's directions
- Uses whole-arm movements to sky-write lines in the air
- Sits at a table to write for very short periods of time

Fine-Motor Skills

- Manipulates small objects, such as blocks, and places them deliberately
- Demonstrates clear preference for one dominant hand
- Reaches across the midline of the body to complete tasks
- When playing, displays strength in hands, fingers, wrists, and elbows
- Grips a writing tool with three fingers
- Uses helper hand to steady paper, puzzle frame, container, or other materials while dominant hand performs task

Spatial Awareness

- Attempts to identify left and right, with frequent errors
- Understands top and bottom
- Identifies vertical (pull down) lines, horizontal (slide) lines, circle lines, and slant lines

Print Awareness

- Understands that written text conveys meaning
- Writes for a variety of purposes that have personal meaning
- Writes during dramatic play
- Knows difference between letters and words
- Shows understanding that writing proceeds across page from left to right

Uppercase Letter Recognition

- Names many uppercase letters, both in and out of alphabetic sequence
- Finds specific uppercase letters in words in the environment
- Names initial letter of his or her first name
- Identifies letters that share similar lines (e.g., points to two or more letters that contain pull down lines)

Uppercase Sound-Symbol Awareness

- Knows sounds of several letters
- Attempts to sound out words in the environment
- Knows sound of initial letter of his or her first name
- Associates pictured words with uppercase letters (e.g., *apple* for **A**)

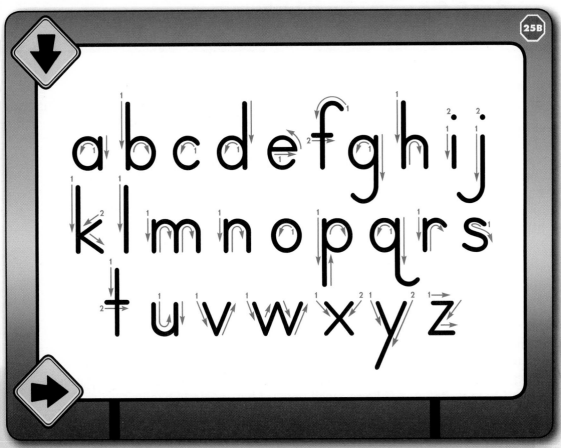

Lowercase Letter Recognition

- Attempts to match uppercase and lowercase letter pairs
- Names several lowercase letters, both in and out of alphabetic sequence
- Finds specific lowercase letters in words in the environment
- Attempts to name lowercase letters in his or her first name
- Identifies letters that share similar lines (e.g., points to two or more letters that contain slide lines)

Lowercase Sound-Symbol Awareness

- Knows sounds of several letters
- Attempts to sound out words in the environment
- Knows sounds of some lowercase letters in his or her first name
- Associates pictured words with lowercase letters (e.g., *apple* for **a**)

Beginning Handwriting Skills

- Writes basic handwriting strokes (pull down/vertical line, slide/horizontal line, circle lines, slant lines)
- Writes letters from top to bottom
- Begins known letters at correct starting point (at green dot)
- Demonstrates correct stroke sequence for writing known letters
- Writes own first name

Glossary

basic strokes: lines that make up all alphabet letters (e.g., vertical, horizontal, circle, slant)

circle back line: counter-clockwise circle that begins at 1:00 position; first stroke in **O, d**

circle forward line: clockwise circle that begins at 9:00 position; second stroke in **b, p**

continuous-stroke manuscript alphabet: Zaner-Bloser alphabet that requires few lifts of the writing tool

directionality: left-to-right and top-to-bottom movement of eyes, hands, and writing tool when reading and writing

fine-motor skills: movements such as grasping, releasing, tearing, cutting, drawing, and writing that depend on development of the small muscles such as those found in the hands and wrists; strength and control of the hand support a child's ability to write

green dot: mark that signals correct starting point for writing a letter with maximum efficiency and ease

grip: method of holding a writing tool; three-finger (tripod) grip is preferred

gross-motor skills: movements such as running, jumping, throwing and catching that depend on development of the large muscles of the body, including those in the arms and legs

hand preference: tendency to choose one dominant and more skilled hand (right or left) for tasks such as writing or throwing a ball

handwriting skills: ability to write—with comfort and efficiency—letters, words, and sentences that can be easily read by others

helper hand: non-dominant or non-writing hand that steadies paper and other materials while dominant hand performs task

left-handed writers: children who display a clear preference for writing with a skilled left hand; left-handers benefit from recognition of their perspective on the writing task

letter recognition: ability to identify each uppercase and lowercase letter character based on its unique shape and visual attributes

letter shape: the unique combination of lines and curves that give each letter a recognizable shape

midline: middle of the body; learning to cross the midline with the dominant hand (rather than switching hands in the middle of a task) is an important prewriting skill

multisensory practice: writing practice that engages visual, auditory, and tactile/kinesthetic learners

perceptual-motor skill: skill, such as handwriting, that equally involves abilities of the mind and body

print awareness: understanding that written words convey important meanings, and that lines of text are arranged from front-to-back, top-to-bottom, and left-to-right

pull down line: vertical line written from top to bottom; first stroke of **T, l**

retrace: point in writing a letter where a previously written line must be retraced; vertical line in **p** must be retraced upward before circle begins

reversal: tendency to confuse letters with mirror-opposite shapes, such as **b** and **d**

shared/interactive writing: writing method in which the teacher transcribes children's words, or seeks their help in supplying words, letters, and spellings while composing a group text

sky-writing: method of using large arm muscles to trace a letter's shape in the air before writing it on paper

slant left line: line that begins at the right and slants down to the left; first stroke in **A**

slant right line: line that begins at the left and slants down to the right; first stroke in **W**

slant up line: line that begins at the left and slants up to the right; second stroke in **W**

slide line: horizontal line written from left to right; first stroke in **e**

sound-symbol awareness: understanding that alphabet letters represent spoken sounds that make up words (e.g., **Bb** for /b/ sound that begins *book*)

spatial awareness: understanding of directional words and concepts such as *up*, *down*, *left*, and *right* that are critical to reading and writing

writing hand: dominant, more skilled hand preferred for tasks such as writing or throwing a ball